FLOWER

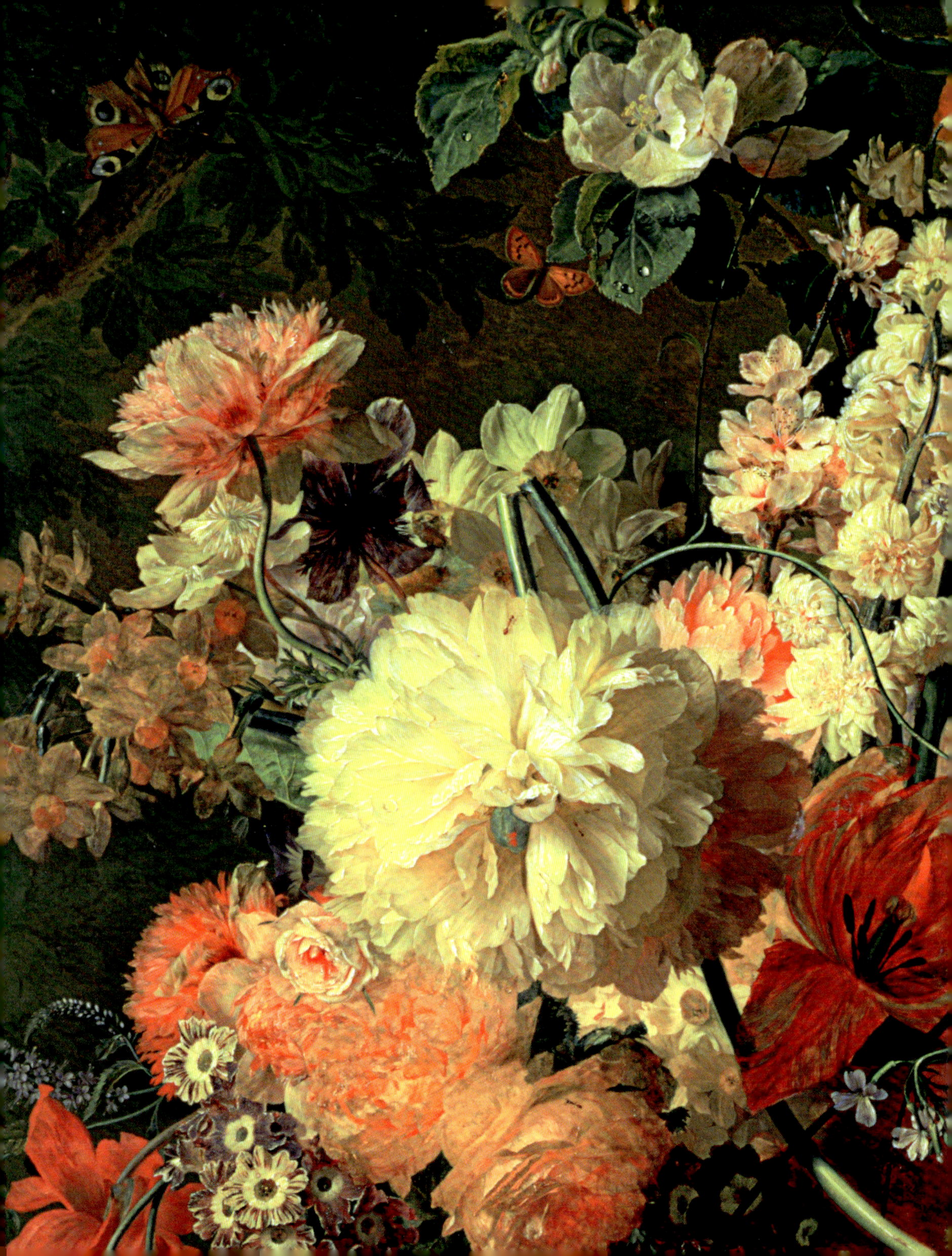

FLOWER

PAINTINGS BY 40 GREAT ARTISTS

CELIA FISHER

FRANCES LINCOLN LIMITED
PUBLISHERS

Frances Lincoln Limited
4 Torriano Mews, Torriano Avenue
London NW5 2RZ
www.franceslincoln.com

Flower: Paintings by 40 Great Artists

First Frances Lincoln edition 2012

A catalogue record for this book is available from the British Library.

978-0-7112-3361-4

Printed and bound in China

1 2 3 4 5 6 7 8 9

Commissioned and edited by Jane Crawley

Front cover: VINCENT VAN GOGH
Almond Blossom (detail) 1890

Back cover: GUSTAVE CAILLEBOTTE
Clump of Chrysanthemums, Garden at Petit Gennevilliers 1893

Title page: JAN VAN HUYSUM
Fowers in a Vase (detail) 1726

Right: PIERRE-AUGUSTE RENOIR
The Garden in the Rue Cortot, Montmartre (detail) 1876

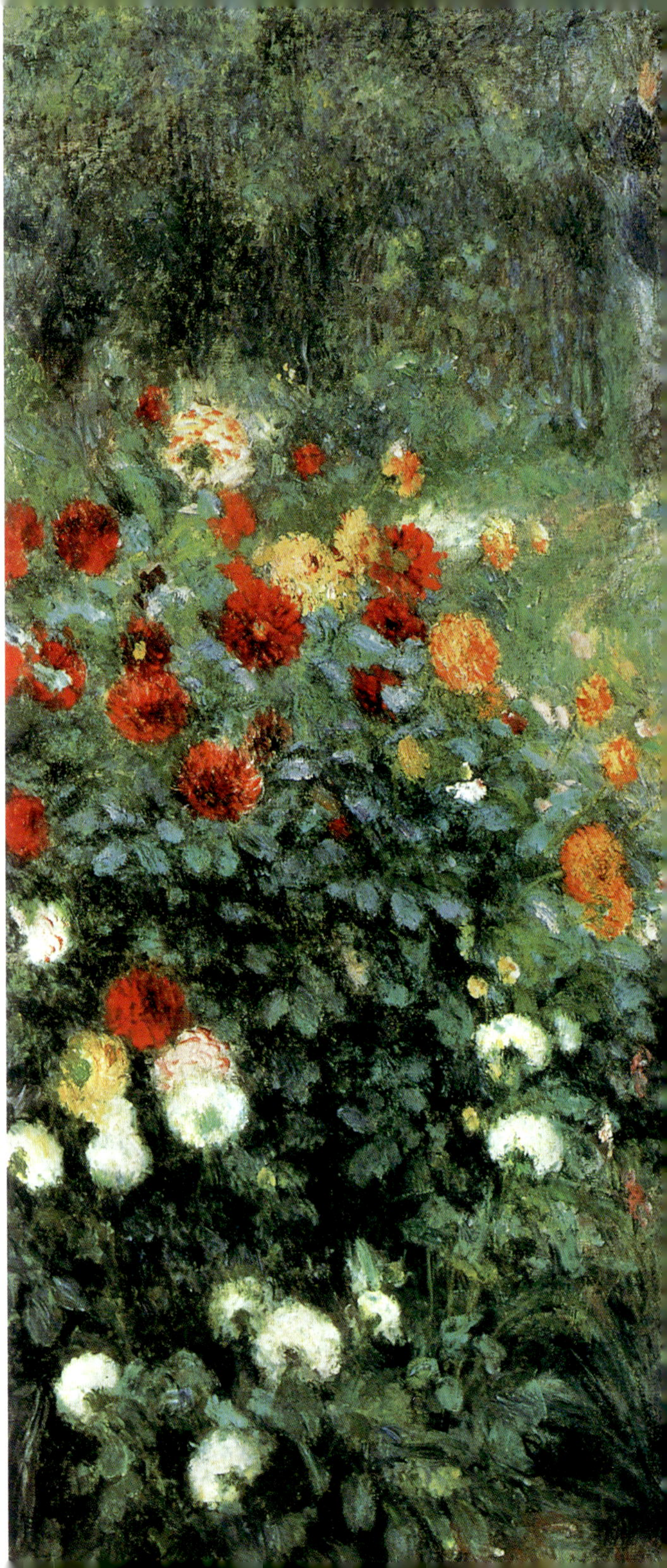

CONTENTS

6 Introduction

14 Albrecht Dürer
16 Ambrosius Bosschaert
18 Jan Brueghel
20 Juan de Arellano
22 Jan Davidz. de Heem
24 Abraham Mignon
26 Rachel Ruysch
28 Jan van Huysum
30 Jiang Yu
32 Katsushika Hokusai
34 Utagawa Hiroshige
36 Martin Johnson Heade
38 Pierre-Auguste Renoir
40 Edouard Manet
42 Marianne North
44 William Morris
46 Vincent Van Gogh
48 Paul Gauguin
50 Gustave Caillebotte
52 Henri Fantin-Latour
54 Paul Cézanne
56 Pablo Picasso
58 Claude Monet
60 Odilon Redon
62 Charles Rennie Mackintosh
64 Henri Rousseau
66 Duncan Grant
68 Matthew Smith
70 Paul Klee
72 Emil Nolde
74 Samuel Peploe
76 Henri Matisse
78 Christopher Wood
80 Vanessa Bell
82 Georgia O'Keeffe
84 Cedric Morris
86 Dorothea Tanning
88 Salvador Dali
90 Gary Hume
92 Elizabeth Blackadder

94 Index
96 Acknowledgements

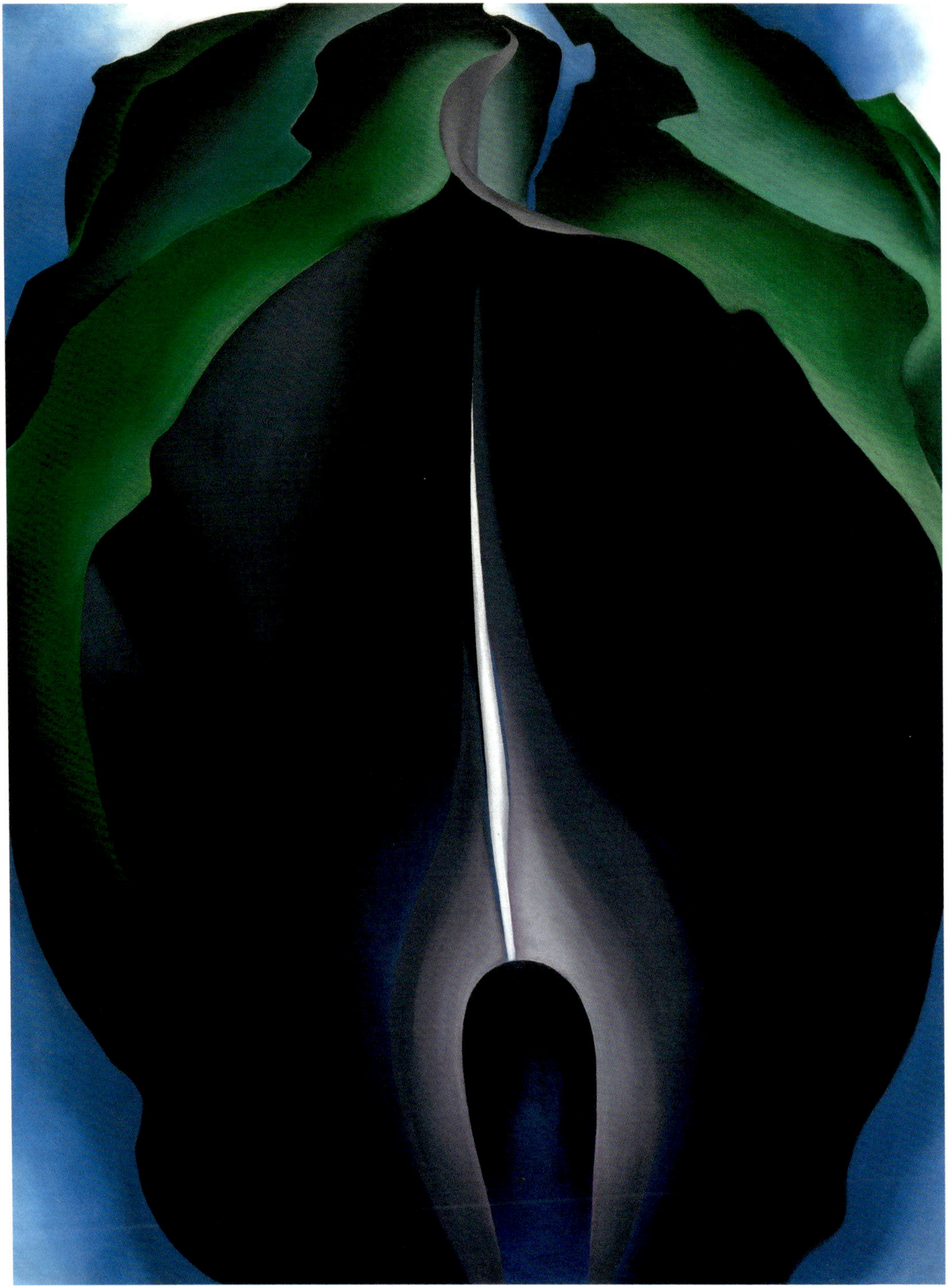

INTRODUCTION

This book is about different ways of looking at flowers – artistically rather than scientifically, but not simply as decoration. The chosen examples represent the art movements of their time, together with something more extreme and passionate coming from the individual artists. Georgia O'Keeffe wrote: 'Nobody sees a flower – really – it is so small – we haven't time – and to see takes time like to have a friend takes time. So I said to myself I'll paint what I see, what the flower is to me, but I'll paint it big and they will be surprised into taking time to look at it.'

O'Keeffe was fascinated by arums (like Diego Rivera who repeatedly painted waxy-white calla lilies). She painted a series of six entitled *Jack-in-the-Pulpit*, each growing increasingly abstract as she zoomed into the centre of the flower. Such dramatic close-ups were also well suited to another sexy flower, the orchid, which is adapted more flamboyantly than most species to waylay pollinating insects, for which purpose it sports protuberances and patterns that also intrigue humans. O'Keeffe chose Brassavola hybrids, and Gary Hume painted slipper orchids, but the trend had begun earlier with the travels of Marianne North, a Victorian lady painter, who set her dramatically enlarged comet orchids among tropical vegetation and butterflies; and with Martin Johnson Heade who journeyed to Central America for inspiration and painted cattleyas looming from jungle landscapes amid humming birds.

They also painted roses; almost everyone from Botticelli to Cy Twombly has painted roses. This book could easily have been of roses alone and through them the history of both art and horticulture could have been traced. For two centuries before flowers actually became the subject of artworks white roses appeared in religious contexts alongside the Virgin Mary to represent her purity and spirituality, while red roses symbolised the redeeming blood of Christ. These were the two traditional roses of Europe, semi-double with their golden stamens glowing in the centre of the flower.

GEORGIA O'KEEFFE
Jack-in-the-Pulpit No. IV 1930
Oil on canvas, 101.6 x 76.2 cm
National Gallery of Art, Washington

Then, early in the seventeenth century, the Spanish artist Zurbaran painted a mystic still life of vessels associated with the Mass, with one damask rose, a species which is white but blushes pink as it opens. This rose may symbolise the Virgin conceiving Christ, or the water in the cup about to be miraculously turned to wine. For rose historians it is above all the portrait of a rose new to European art.

Zurbaran's still life was unusual in featuring one flower, artists of the seventeenth century generally favoured quantity as well as quality and, among the latest novelties to appear in flower paintings, roses earned a central position. Mignon included the many-petalled *centifolia* rose (the pride of rose breeders), the even newer bicoloured rose and a single yellow rose, while van Huysum's rarest flower was a double yellow rose. Some symbolism remained – among these exquisite petals insects rummaged as a reminder of mortality (the same preoccupation that the contemporary artist Marc Quinn seeks to express with his silicon flowers frozen in a false, perpetual bloom). The diversity of rose symbolism grows with every century and becomes more enigmatic – Manet's rose in a brioche, Klee's rose garden and Dali's surreal red rose suspended in a blue sky.

The idea of painting flowers against the sky first arrived in Europe from Japan with woodcut

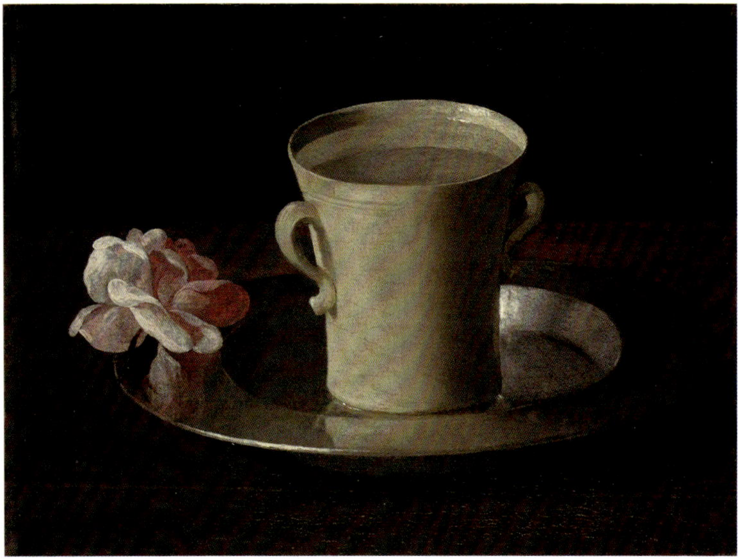

FRANCISCO DE ZURBARAN
A Cup of Water and a Rose c.1630
Oil on canvas, 21.2 x 30.1 cm
National Gallery, London

ABRAHAM MIGNON
Flowerpiece (detail) c.1670
Oil on panel, 50.8 x 36.8 cm
Fitzwilliam Museum, University of Cambridge

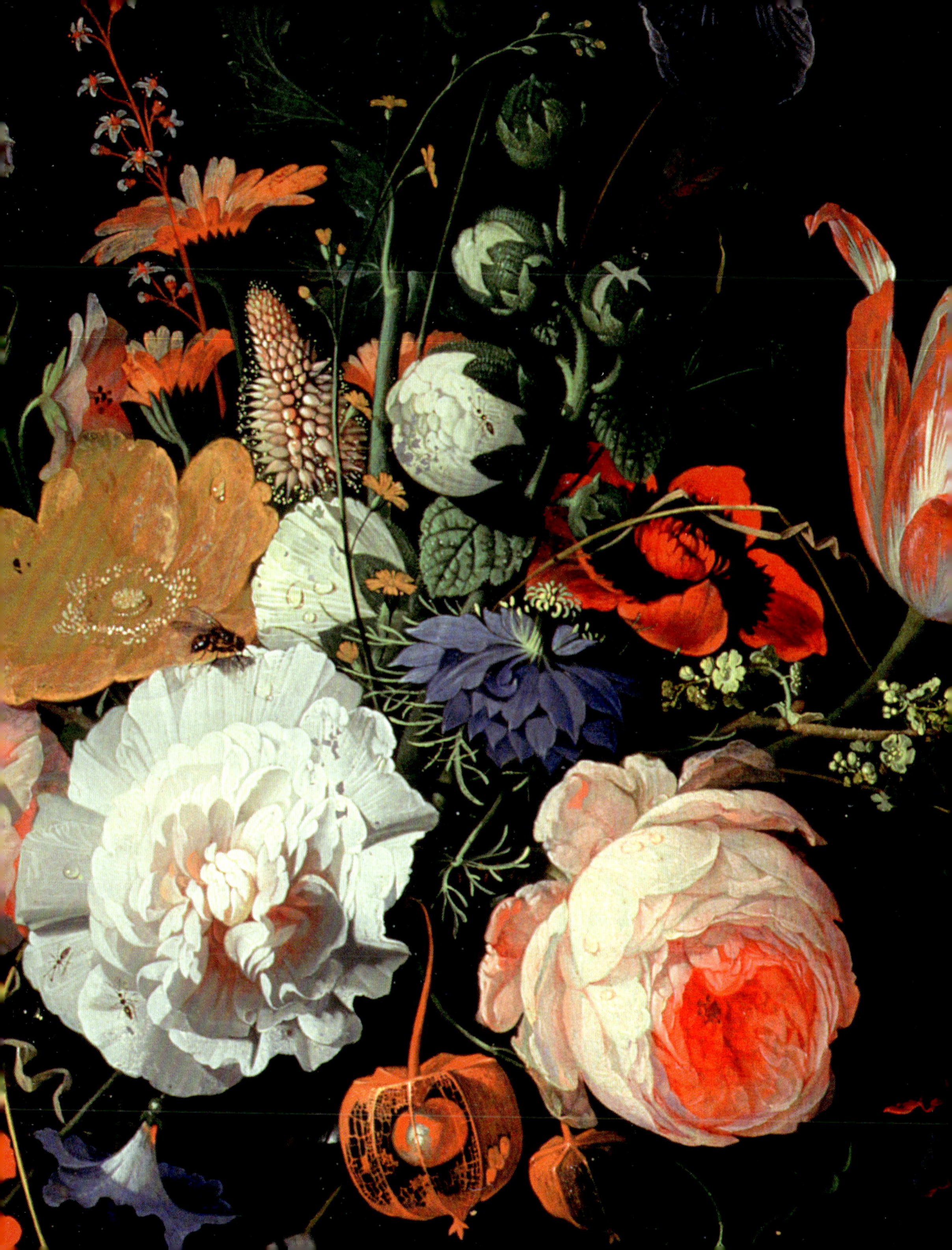

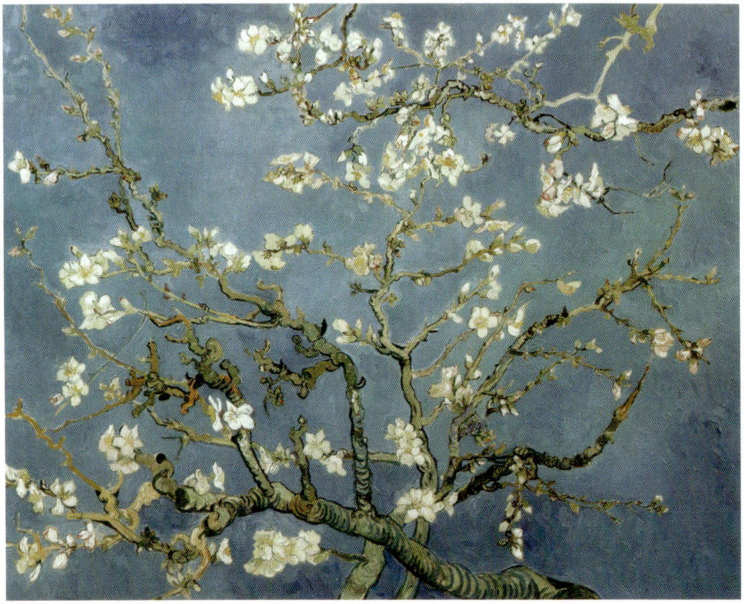

VINCENT VAN GOGH
Almond Blossom 1890
Oil on canvas, 73.5 x 92 cm
Van Gogh Museum, Amsterdam

prints, just in time to inspire the Impressionists in the use of different viewpoints and bold blocks of colour. Otherwise Renoir might never have stared diagonally downwards on a bed of dahlias, nor Caillebotte crouched among his chrysanthemums, nor Monet gazed across the watery expanses of his lily ponds allowing the sky to appear only in reflection. But the sky itself was Van Gogh's, whether he was painting starry constellations, dark crows or branches of spring blossom. He was so fascinated by Japanese art that he copied Hiroshige's print of the *Plum Garden at Kameido* (and his *Bridge in the Rain*) and tried to absorb the philosophy behind them. Above all there was the question of reality, a challenge for every generation of artists – because inevitably they deal in illusions.

In the West the bias of flower painting had (until the Impressionist movement) been towards achieving scientific accuracy, while in the East the artist's skill lay in capturing the sense that the plant was alive – as Dylan Thomas put it: 'the force that through the green fuse drives the flower'. This was not necessarily done by observation, rather by a lifetime of seeking harmony with nature, refining the necessary techniques and the discipline of endless repetition, in order to achieve perfect self-expression.

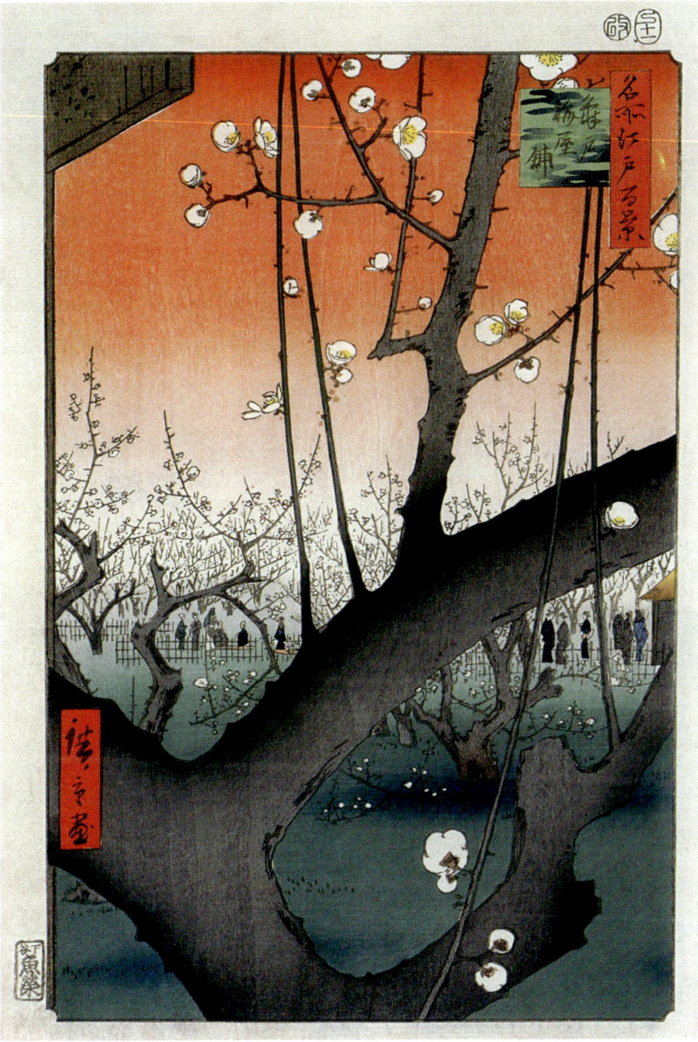

This may help to explain how flower painters as diverse as Van Gogh, Charles Rennie Mackintosh and Elizabeth Blackadder all emulated the energy and refinement of Japanese aesthetics. While for Monet the idea of creating a series of the same subject in varying conditions, which led finally to his lily ponds, owed much to Japanese prints grouped under titles such as *One Hundred Views of Edo*. The wisteria which he painted as his eyesight failed, in abstract calligraphic patterns but still unmistakeably wisteria, was Japanese both in origin and style.

Above all, Japanese prints helped to release colour from the confines of straightforward imitation. This was the context in which Gauguin as well as Matisse, and even Picasso, were influenced by Japanese prints, and became extravagant with colour in a manner loosely termed Symbolist. When a seventeenth-century artist like Jan Brueghel painted a cyclamen, it was a tiny delicate thing among a great arrangement, or else placed on a ledge beside a central vase as a

UTAGAWA HIROSHIGE
One Hundred Views of Edo: The Plum Garden at Kameido 1856
Colour woodblock print, 36.8 x 25 cm
Tokyo Fuji Art Museum, Tokyo

wondrous little botanical specimen complete with its rooty corm. When Matisse painted a cyclamen it was a triumph of pink against blue, large, startling and vibrant. Although Matisse's version was less realistic he demanded more strongly that one consider the flower itself. Similarly when Bosschaert painted a tulip, the streaks of colour that made it fabulously expensive were exquisitely and precisely defined, but when Duncan Grant painted tulips their vitality sang out from the canvas in a blur of colour. Matisse and his followers opened the way for a purely abstract artist like Patrick Heron who described entering a greenhouse and seeing 'a violet flower with five petals suspended against the receptive furry green leaves' as 'the terrific zing of a violet vibration'. One suspects the flower was an African violet, the words describing it are superb, but alas with abstraction the individual flowers are quite lost. This was the risk inherent in Kandinsky's belief that 'colour and form should no longer be indebted to outward appearances in nature but to the feelings and inner world of the artist'.

HENRI MATISSE
Purple Cyclamen 1911–12
Oil on canvas, 73 x 60 cm
Private collection

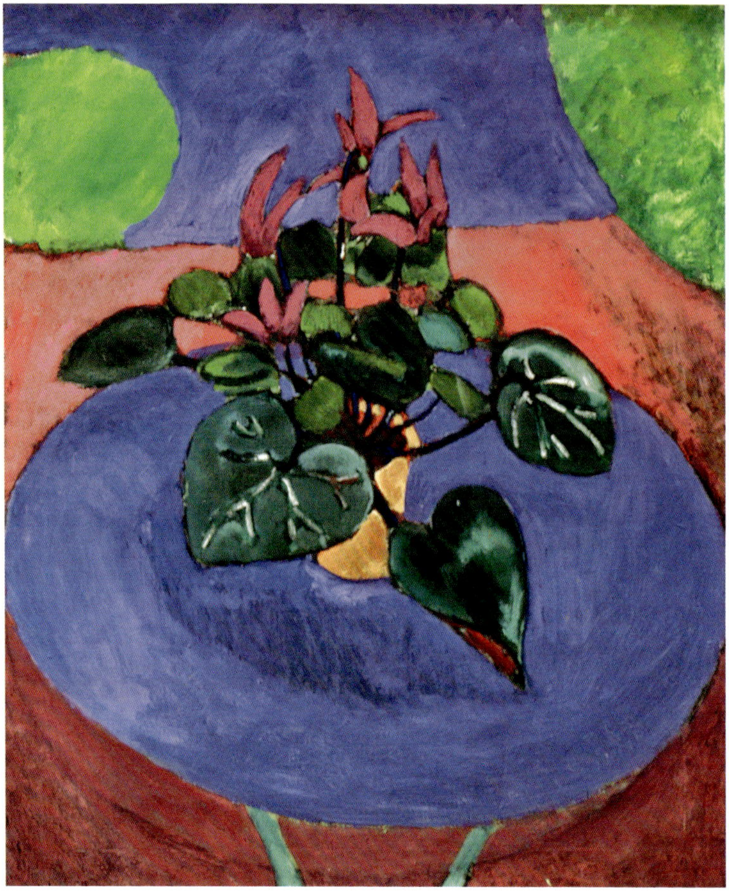

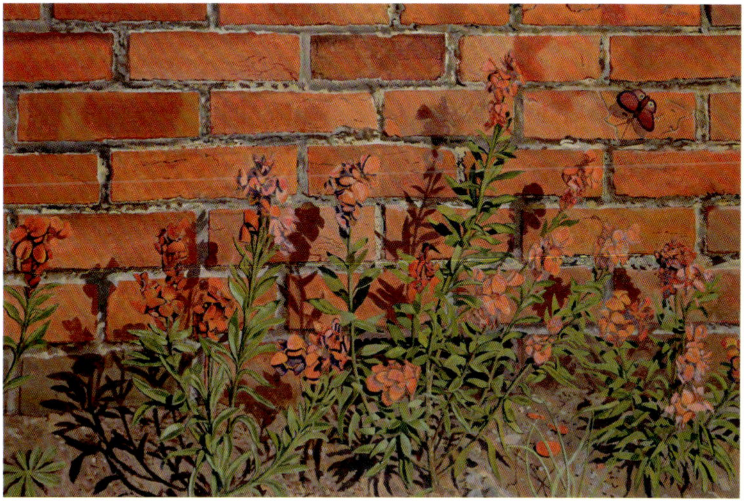

But modern art contains many traditions and often makes reference to the art of the past. When Howard Hodgkin painted a lotus flower with a brush full of green paint, simply forming a V shape against green rectangles, he described the place in India where they grew as a 'Douanier Rousseau garden', which helped to add a humid jungle atmosphere to the flowers he sought to evoke. When the Surrealist painter Dorothea Tanning used a sunflower as a threatening image was she expecting everyone to think of Van Gogh's sunflowers? Which brings the questions surrounding artists' flowers back to roses, and whether Dali meant his surreal red rose to be a celestial or a sexual symbol.

Flowers continue to exercise a powerful spell and to be full of hidden meaning, but for those who prefer them less abstract and less complicated, Stanley Spencer was heroic in his simplicity. He placed flowers back among the earth and walls of cottage gardens, happy and sensitive in the warm light. His loving description of snowdrops waiting to be painted could apply to any flower: 'They were fearfully pleased with themselves. You could imagine them discussing it.... "he's come right to where we are with a camp stool, there's something up...I knew there was something about us".'

STANLEY SPENCER
Wallflowers 1954
Oil on canvas, 49.5 x 74.9 cm
Private collection

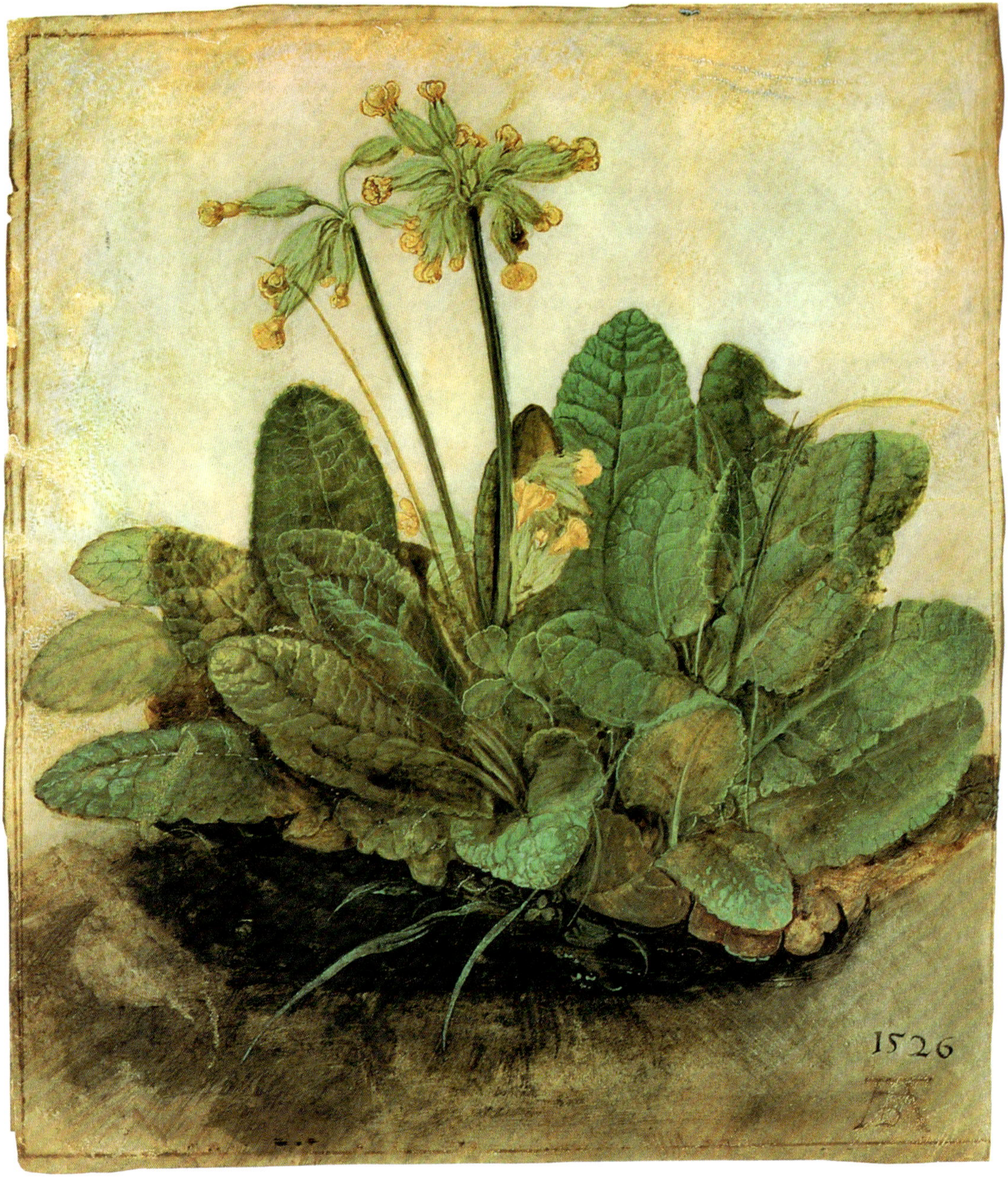

Tuft of Cowslips 1526
Gouache on vellum, 19.3 x 16.8 cm
National Gallery of Art, Washington,
Armand Hammer Collection

ALBRECHT DÜRER (1471–1528)

Cowslips

In the countryside, where cowslips once grew abundantly, their honeyed yellow flowers were plucked for cowslip wine, a gentle narcotic much valued for pains and palsies. The clustered flowers hanging from the stem were thought to resemble bunches of tiny keys. According to the myths of northern Europe cowslips were dedicated to the goddess Freya and believed to open the way to her treasure palace. With Christianity the symbolism was transferred to St Peter, whose emblem was the key that gave entry to heaven, and the German folk name for cowslips, *himmelsschlüssel* (key flower), was part of this tradition.

Dürer was primarily a painter of great religious altarpieces, bringing the realism of the Italian Renaissance to Germany, and as he grew in stature so did the size of his workshop and the number of assistants processing his studies and engravings. When he made his exquisite watercolours of flowers he chose those that appeared in religious scenes. Some, like his irises, can be matched to his paintings (or those of his followers) and the rest were all of plants typically found in images of the Virgin and Child in a flowery setting. The cowslips (like Dürer's columbine and patch of turf) were depicted still rooted in soil, perhaps to reinforce a message that the flowers formed a spiritual link between heaven and earth. But, more pragmatically, this would have kept them alive for observation; Dürer was among the founding fathers of botanical illustration, making scientifically accurate studies from life – indeed he may have trained Hans Weiditz, who in 1521 produced the first lifelike illustrations for a printed herbal, transforming the old stylised traditions of representing flowers.

Dürer is also known to have treasured a watercolour of a peony by Martin Schongauer dated 1472 which was the model for the peony in his altarpiece of the *Virgin and Child in a Rose Bower*. This pushes back into the fifteenth century the time when artists first looked at flowers with botanists' eyes in order to bring their art closer to truth.

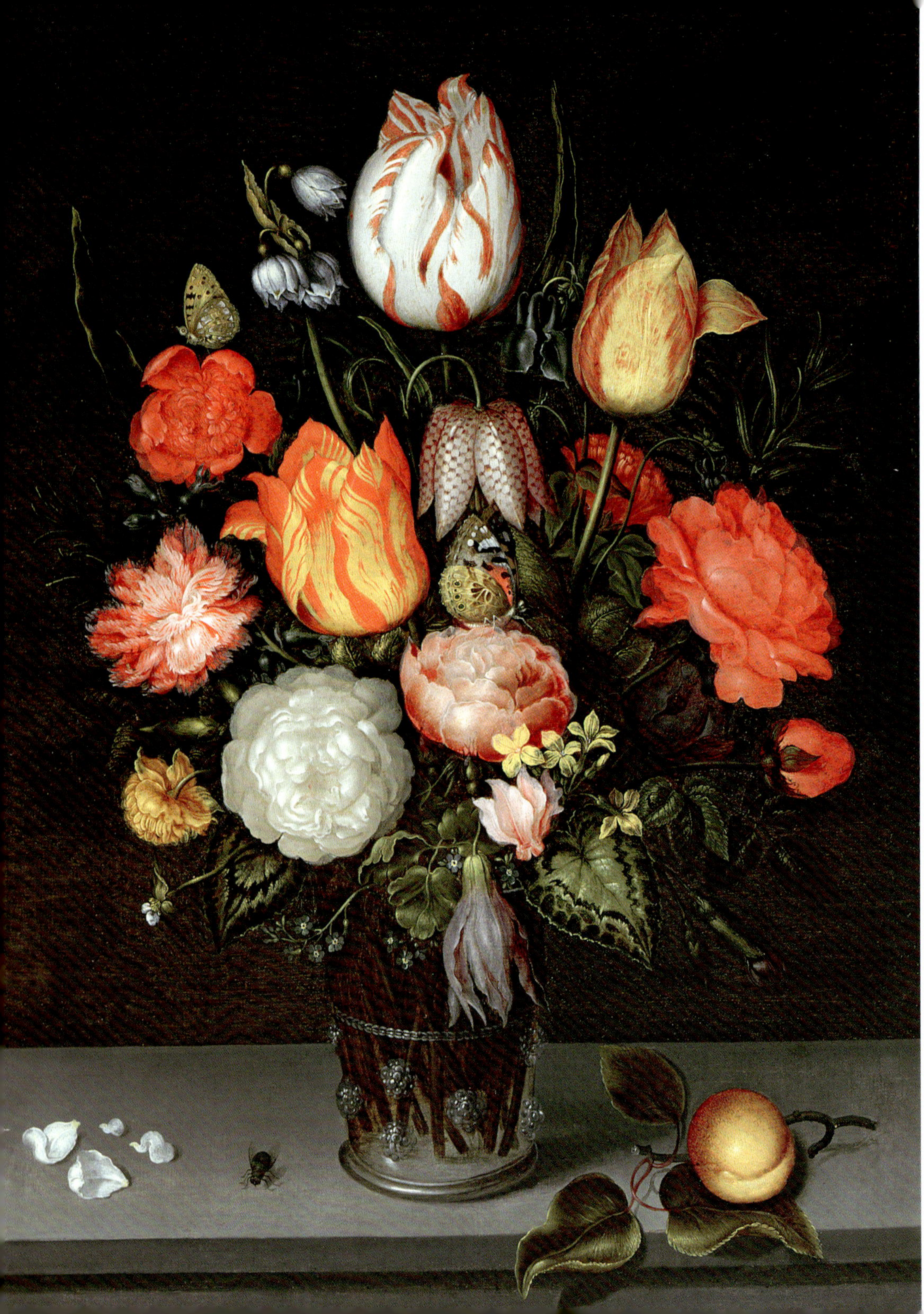

AMBROSIUS BOSSCHAERT
(1573–1621)

Still Life with Fruit and Flowers c.1615
Oil on canvas, 45.5 x 33.5 cm
Private collection

Tulips, fritillary and other flowers

Ambrosius Bosschaert represents the first moment when flowers became the subject of paintings in their own right, rather than being part of a scene animated by people. The impetus for this was the introduction of exotic new plants and the fever of interest they aroused – none as much as tulips, and nowhere comparable to Holland, where Bosschaert made his career after fleeing from Catholic persecution in Antwerp early in the 1590s. Bosschaert founded a successful dynasty of painters and dealers working in Utrecht; but during his lifetime collectors and speculators were exchanging tulips for ever larger sums, and eventually one bulb might have cost ten times the price of his painting. Which means this was no flower arrangement in the normal sense, but the artist's composition made from separate studies of rare individual blooms.

The 'top flower' in Bosschaert's vase (where he created a tradition of setting the most prized above the rest) looks like the legendary 'Semper Augustus', the most expensive tulip of all time, which was white with rose markings. Beneath are the bizarres, the red and yellow tulips, one 'flamed' with red streaks in the centre of the petals, the other 'feathered' with red around the edges of the petals. These patterns of vivid and unpredictable colour (caused, though no one realised, by a virus) gave the tulips their fascination and their value; and while confidence remained prices mounted, but in 1637 the market crashed, giving tulips a place in economic as well as art history.

Possibly Bosschaert prophesied this by placing a drooping, chequered fritillary among the gaudy tulips. The sense of chance, if not doom, was reflected in their name, likening the shape of the flowers to a dice box, which in Latin is *fritillus*. Such warning messages, known as *vanitas*, were well known in seventeenth-century still lifes and they reappear on the ledge with the fallen petals and the fly.

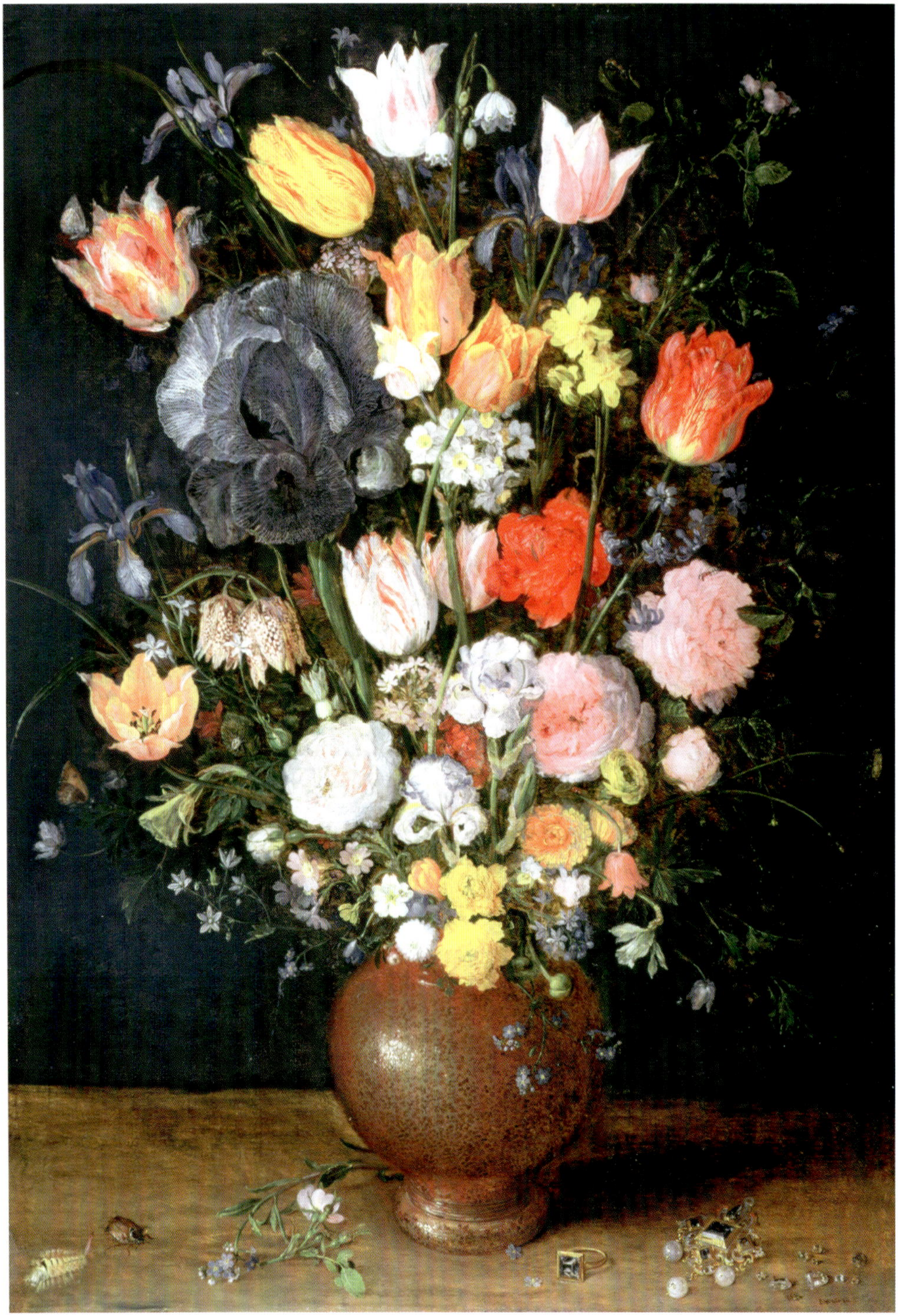

JAN BRUEGHEL (1568–1625)

Irises, tulips, narcissi and other flowers

Jan Brueghel in Antwerp was, like Bosschaert in Utrecht, a founder of flower painting in the Netherlands. Unlike his brother Pieter, who imitated the work of their father Pieter Brueghel the Elder, Jan concentrated on flower and garden themes and created a style that was not only different but inimitable. Where Bosschaert and his followers painted flowers like enamelled jewels, Brueghel's brushwork had a melting softness, perfect for rendering the fragility of petals and the translucence of their colours. His work was artificial in the most generous sense, since he assembled impossibly large quantities of flowers, clustering the tiny ones like snowdrops, violas, cyclamen and primulas at the rim of the vase while the larger blooms soared upwards to dramatic heights. In this painting the silken, summer roses support an edifice of spring flowers, a spiral of tulips, several unusual species of narcissi and a halo of blue hyacinths and irises.

The irises are alpine species, not the traditional flag iris of European gardens, but shy flowers new to cultivation and much smaller, making the improbable length that Brueghel added to his stems even more apparent. High in the composition he has captured the horizontal spread of *Iris xiphium*, the slender petals of *Iris reticulata* and the heavy, rounded flower of *Iris susiana* with its veined patterns. Surprising that two lovely bearded iris, bicoloured blue and white, are lower in the vase among the smaller flowers; providing another clue that Brueghel grouped his flowers together from individual studies made earlier in sketchbooks, risking a loss of proportion, though not of detail, during the transfer to his oil paintings.

Like those of his friend Rubens, Brueghel's paintings are opulent (his nickname was 'Velvet Brueghel') and jewels lie scattered beside the vase. He once asked a cardinal 'whether these flowers do not surpass gold and jewels?' But the predatory creepy crawlies may be a reminder of the churchman's answer that neither flowers nor jewels endure like treasure in heaven.

A Stoneware Vase of Flowers c.1608
Oil on panel, 60.3 x 42.2 cm
Fitzwilliam Museum, University of Cambridge

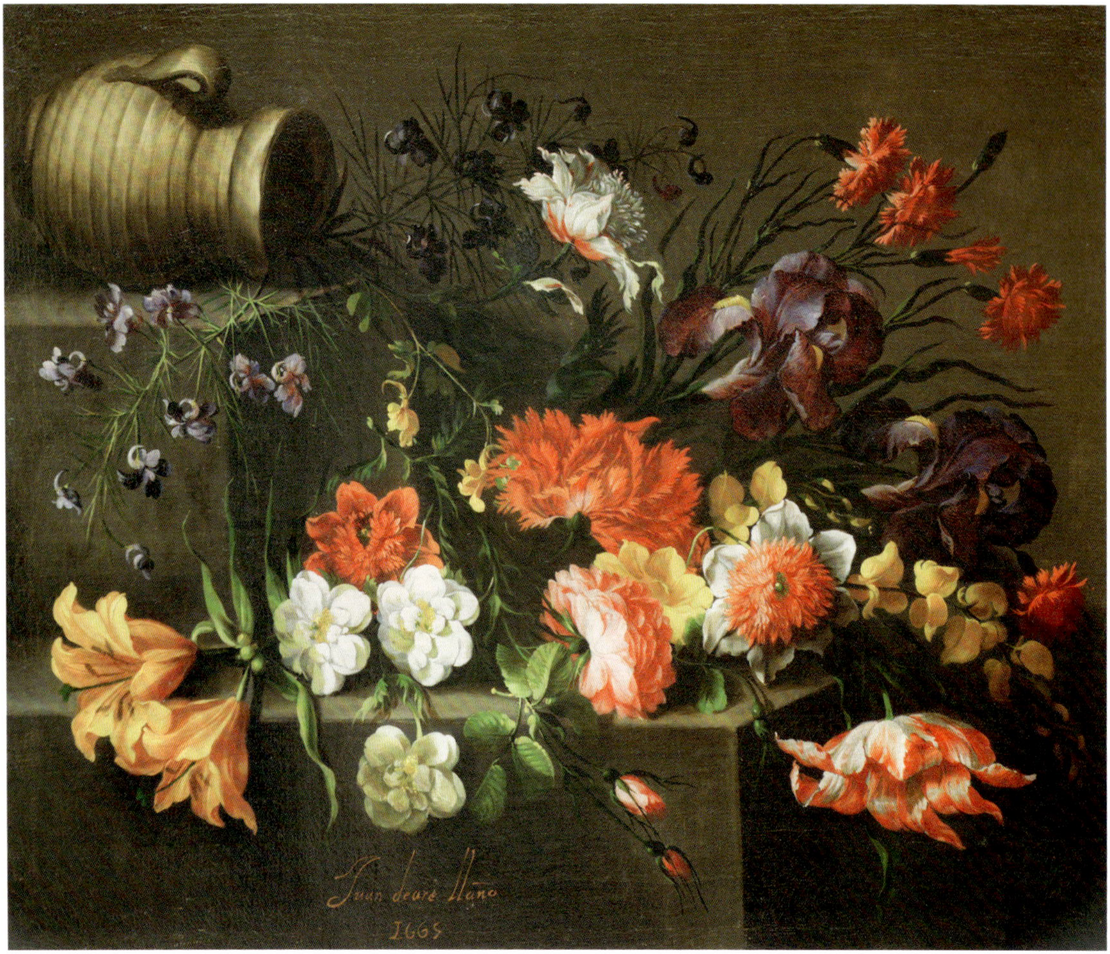

Flowers on a Ledge 1665
Oil on canvas, 63 x 75.5 cm
Private collection

JUAN DE ARELLANO (1614–76)

Lilies, larkspurs and other flowers

By the 1640s when Juan de Arellano first started painting flowers, Madrid's appetite had been whetted by the great Flemish masters, especially Jan Brueghel and Daniel Seghers, who produced Saints and Virgins framed by garlands of flowers for the Catholic market. Heavy masses of flowers fitted well in baroque churches and gilded Spanish drawing rooms, and during the 1650s Arellano turned from painting devotional pictures, declaring that with flowers one could earn more with less effort. He established the largest artist's workshop in the Calle Mayor of Madrid, employing a succession of relatives, collaborators and apprentices all copying his style. His wealth was based on a successful formula – substantial canvases in pairs, or larger series, designed to decorate sumptuous rooms – showing massed flowers in openwork baskets as if just picked and waiting to be arranged, or in bulbous glass vases reflecting strong light and ruffled by a breeze. These were often destined to hang over doors, and presumably in correct relation to the real light and breeze from the windows. Arellano's mature style became more Italianate, since handsome decor paintings needed strong compositional colouring rather than the loving botanical details characteristic of Dutch and Flemish flower paintings.

However some Arellano paintings showed more individual style. A pair dated 1665 has the flowers spilling over a ledge from an overturned pitcher, amusing, inventive and superbly composed. Here, the golden lilies, like bells, are a summons into the sweep of other flowers. Their yellow is balanced by the snapdragons. The sculptural folds of their petals are echoed in the irises which (with a hint of yellow) provide a deep blue contrast. The blue theme circles gracefully into the larkspurs drifting over the upper ledge, as if the flowers might really still be falling. The central pink and white anemones, with roses and a double poppy, cannot help being static, but Arellano's well-honed skill with the breeze effect causes the background red carnations to sway, and the foreground tulip to flutter its petals most convincingly; bringing life, even laughter, into the painting.

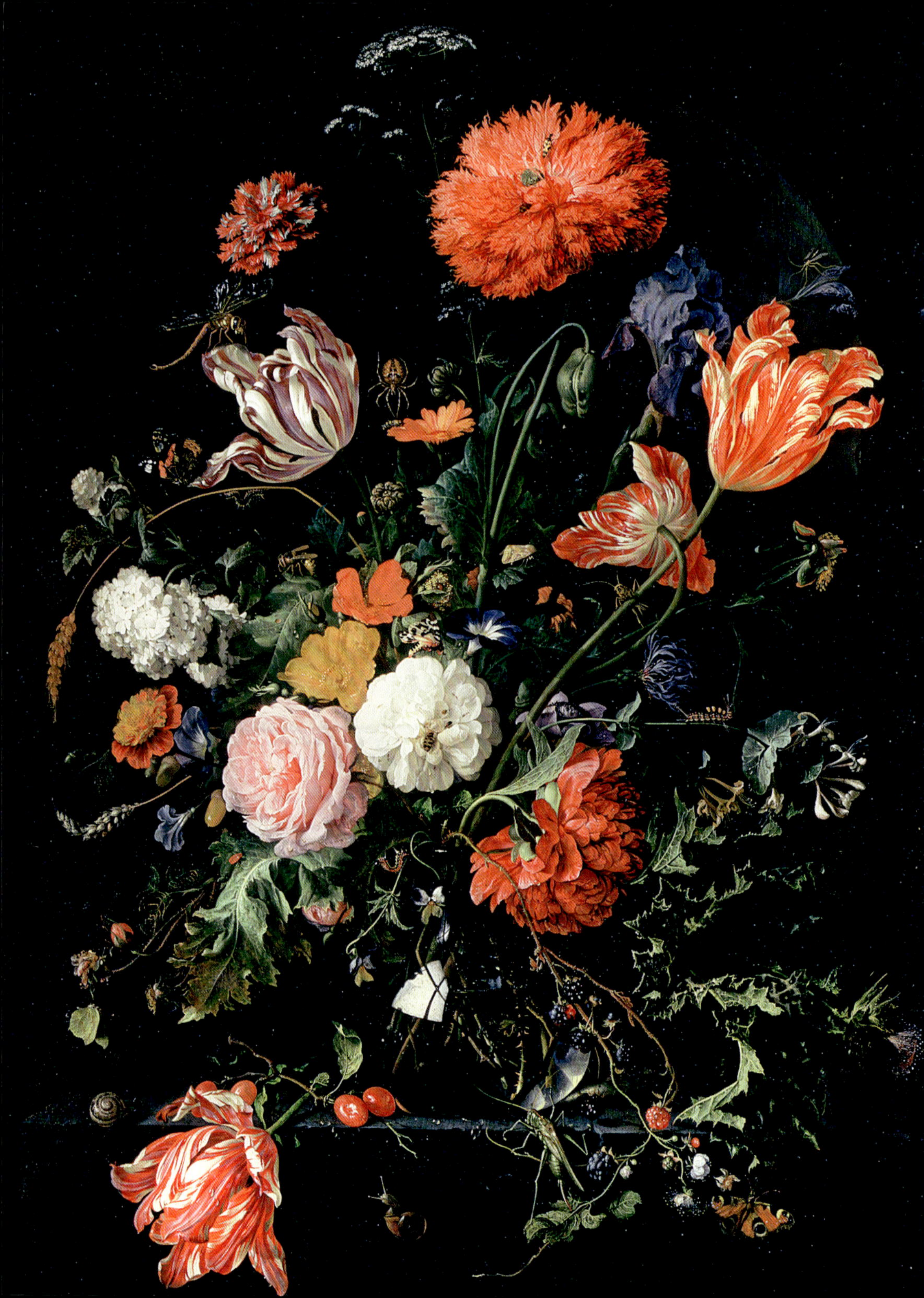

JAN DAVIDSZ. DE HEEM (1606–84)

Tulips, roses, poppy, peony and other flowers

The panache of Jan Davidsz. de Heem dominated flower painting in the Netherlands during the second half of the seventeenth century, as Bosschaert and Jan Brueghel had done in the first half, and indeed he was heir to both. Starting in Utrecht (like Bosschaert, his Protestant parents had fled from Antwerp), he learnt to paint flowers with precision. As a young man he moved to Leyden where his contemporary Rembrandt was revolutionising the paint effects of light and darkness. And in 1636 he returned to Antwerp, city of wealthy patrons and banqueting rooms, where an artist could grow rich painting decorative swags of flowers – the larger the better – and in size as well as vitality de Heem surpassed all his predecessors.

In this flowerpiece, the influence of painting festoons is evident in de Heem's splendid diagonal sweep from red tulip to red tulip. Their vivid streaks are balanced by the even more dramatic purple and white tulip, while the reds in the painting are centred by the topmost poppy and beneath it the equally double peony drooping over the vase. De Heem's fascination with light is manifested in the reflections in the glass vase, exquisitely suggesting roundness, and possibly a spiritual symbolism in the translucent vessel which contains the flowers and around which they revolve. The light itself creates another diagonal, touching the white streaks on the purple tulip, highlighting the white rose and the guelder rose, until its reflection fades into the vase.

As well as the powerful contrast between light and dark, there is another between cultivated and wild plants: between the softly folded petals of the roses and the bramble lying on the ledge; between the magnificent florists' flowers and the grasses, acorns, hips and honeysuckle from the hedgerows; between the unnaturally patterned petals of the carnation and tulips and the natural colour contrasts of the tiny wild violas. Above all, the teeming insects, did they proclaim the wonders of God's creation or the darker side of life?

Flowers in a Glass Vase c.1670
Oil on panel, 93.2 x 69.8 cm
Fitzwilliam Museum, University of Cambridge

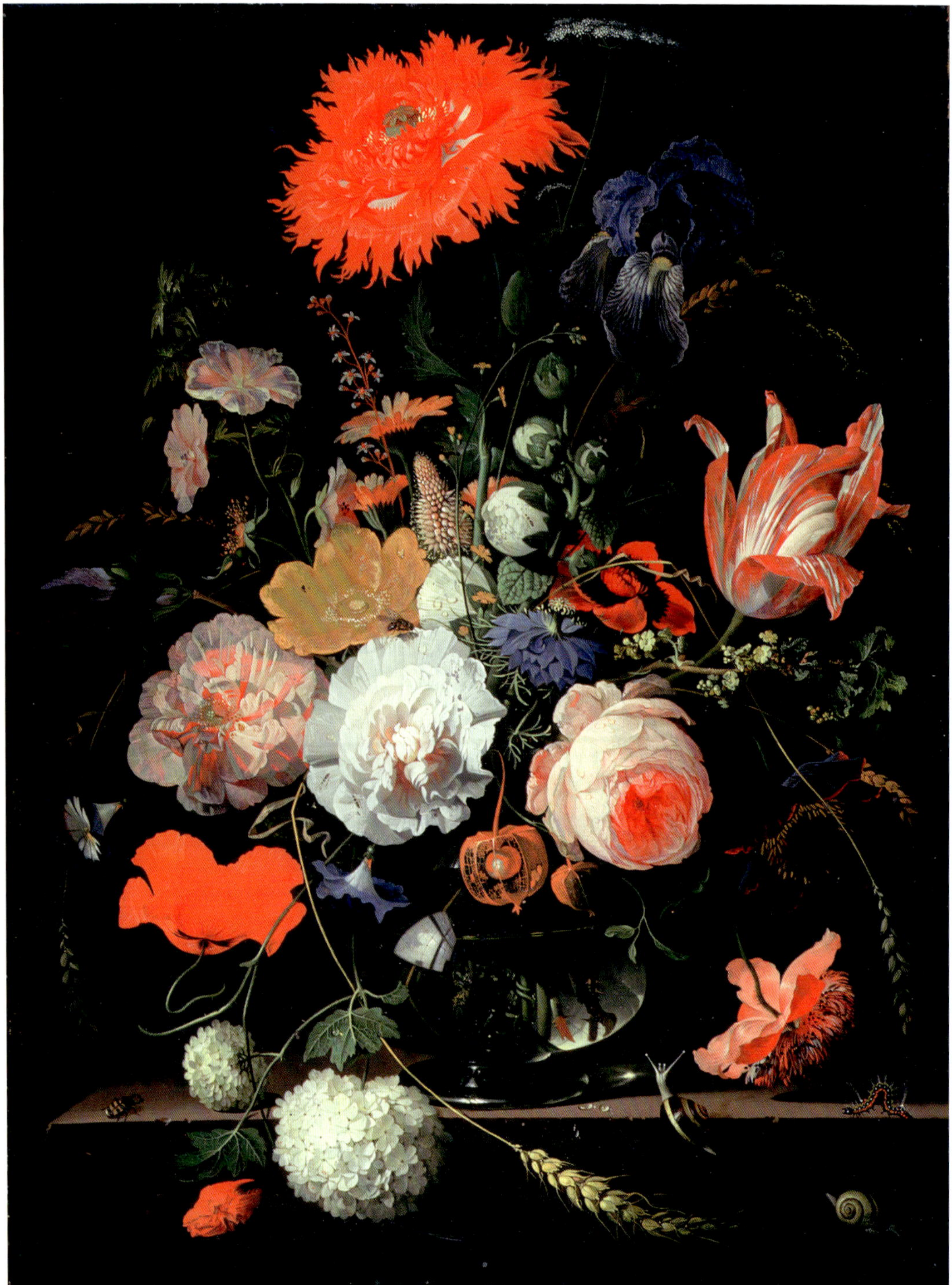

ABRAHAM MIGNON (1640–79)

Roses and other flowers

Most seventeenth-century still lifes which seem to celebrate sensual delights contain a message of transience, and many of Mignon's paintings have more threatening symbols than advancing snails and caterpillars (such as skulls and hourglasses), because behind these paintings of material objects lay religious beliefs that were still intense. Mignon's Calvinist parents had fled from the southern Netherlands into exile in Frankfurt. There Mignon was apprenticed to Jacob Marrell, who in 1659 travelled with him to Utrecht, the great centre of Dutch flower painting. Both master and pupil were much influenced by Jan Davidz. de Heem (who worked in Utrecht as well as Antwerp) and both continued to move between Holland and Germany.

Although he lacked de Heem's spontaneous flair, Mignon imitated him to good effect and his choice of flowers was varied. Around the cacophony of central colour, thistles and thorn apples might lurk in the shadows, as well as the wheat stalks that were typical of de Heem. Emerging from the penumbra (and balancing the only tulip) is a delicate pink geranium, and there is more pink in the unexpected spike of bistort. Hanging over the glass vase with its mirrored sky, a little orange lantern of physalis contains a berry which also reflects the light.

It was customary for artists to enhance the illusion of recession with blue flowers; here a curve passes upwards through the painting – morning glory, nigella and a tall blue iris – each one juxtaposed to red flowers and climaxing in the exploding petals of the topmost poppy.

At the heart of it all the roses steal the show. The central rose beams white light on the hollyhock and guelder rose (so that even a fly casts a shadow). The single yellow rose (a colour previously unknown in European roses) was *Rosa foetida*, a Persian rose introduced via Austria. The double pink rose, aptly named *Rosa centifolia*, was a new hybrid highly prized for its innumerable petals. Also new to cultivation in the seventeenth century was *Rosa mundi*, which had pink and white markings on its petals, giving it the same rarity value as streaked tulips and carnations.

Flowerpiece c.1670
Oil on panel, 50.8 x 36.8 cm
Fitzwilliam Museum, University of Cambridge

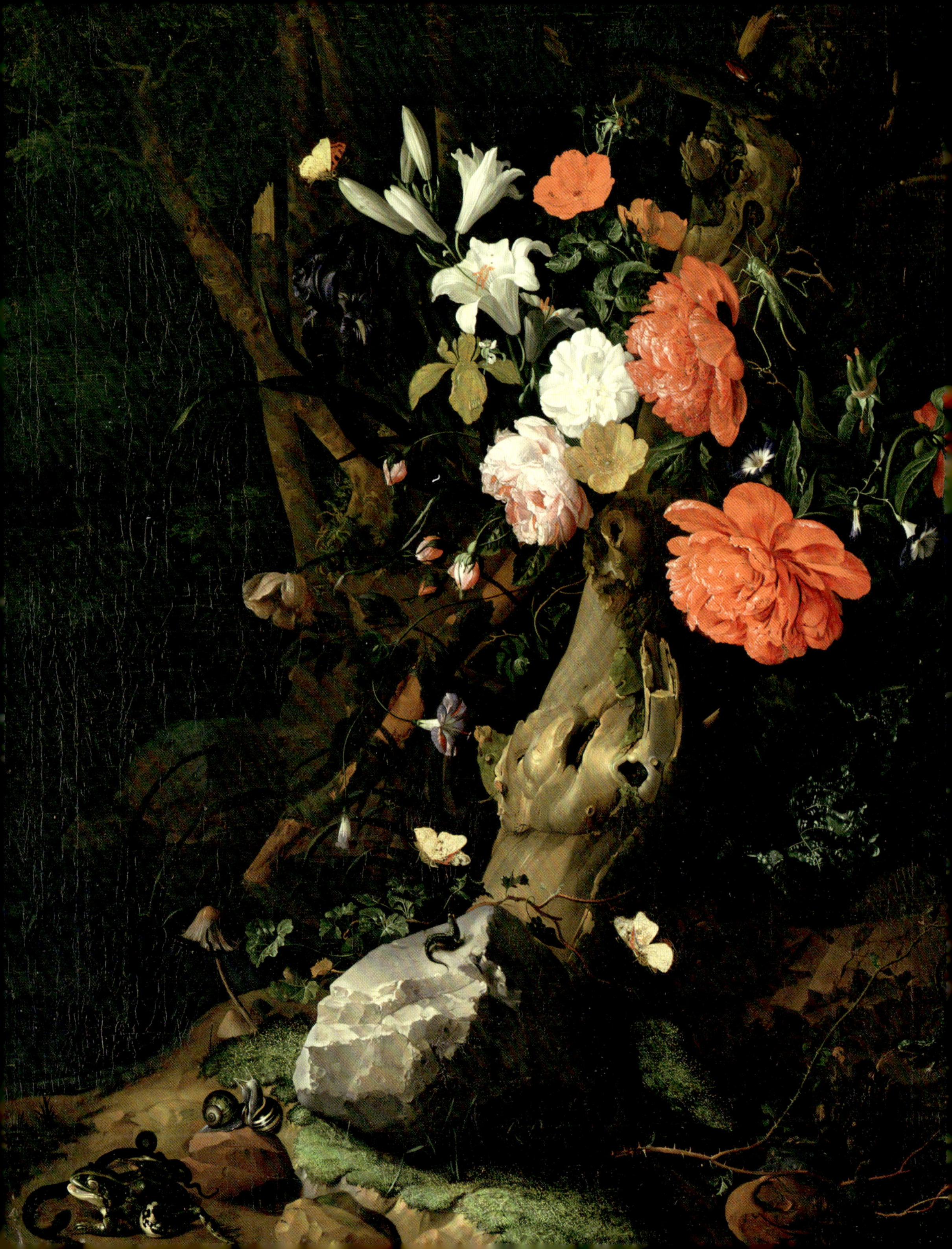

RACHEL RUYSCH (1664–1750)

Lilies, roses, peonies, morning glory and other flowers

The paintings known as 'forest floors' were dark, reptilian scenes enlivened by flowers and butterflies, which grew astonishingly popular from the 1670s and provided artists, including the young Rachel Ruysch, with an excuse to dispense with conventional vases. They were invented by the Dutch artist Otto Marseus van Schrieck, who died in 1678 bequeathing his heirs a trunk full of 'small dead animals'. Rachel's own father, Frederick Ruysch, professor of anatomy and botany, owned a spectacular collection of skeletons and preserved organs, which (like other 'cabinets of curiosities' containing zoological specimens) could be viewed by the interested public of Amsterdam. These scientific displays also inspired Maria Sybilla Merian, another eminent female artist, who juxtaposed insects and flowers and sought to understand their relationships.

The seventeenth-century fascination with reptiles and insects was above all scientific, and to this artists responded, in the same way that their attention to detail imitated a scientist's observational powers. But these 'forest floor' paintings also contrived to be 'vanitas' symbols of light and dark and moral versus material values. Imaginative overload transformed the woodland into an enchanted glade where cherished blooms burst from stumps of rotten wood, and toads and toadstools suggested the ingredients of a witch's brew (and Ruysch probably knew that the morning glories were hallucinogenic). But in these sinister surroundings the lilies, roses and peonies retained their traditional religious associations of purity and spirituality all the more vigorously.

Later in her career Rachel Ruysch abandoned 'forest floors' and concentrated on vases of flowers, which were distinguished by her mellow colours, as if bathed in sunset light, and by her mastery of spatial arrangement (the enchanted glades had played their part in this). She was extremely successful, supporting her husband (who abandoned portrait painting) and ten children, and for a while moving to Germany as court painter to the Elector Palatine. She lived to a ripe age and – which is interesting – her contemporaries were not surprised that a woman could achieve so much.

Still Life of Flowers on Woodland Ground c.1690
Oil on canvas, 93 x 74 cm
Gemäldegalerie, Kassel

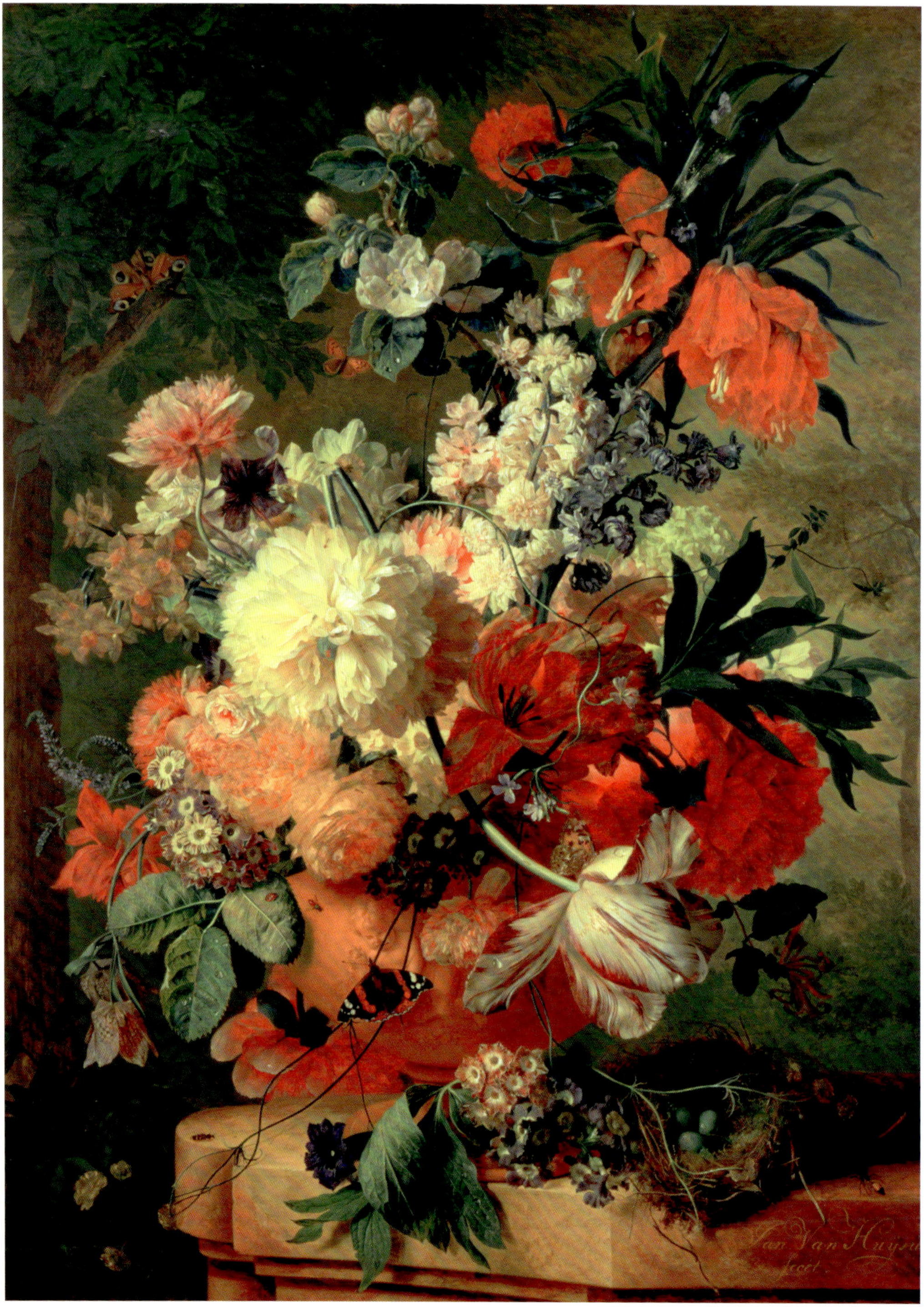

JAN VAN HUYSUM (1682–1749)

Crown imperial, anemones, auriculas and other flowers

The curvaceous swirls of Jan van Huysum's paintings fitted perfectly into the gilded rococo interiors of the eighteenth century, but he placed his flowers outdoors, grouped in great terracotta pots on marble ledges just as growing flowers might be; and a sun-dappled, tree-lined vista, receding behind them, heralded the landscape garden movement. Gone were the dark backgrounds and formal lines of his predecessors, although he did retain some old tricks, such as placing the same flowers at different angles in several paintings, and allowing ants to rummage through the petals of his choicest double blooms.

The massive orange fritillary with its impressive topknot (which earned it the name Crown imperial) was a van Huysum favourite for heading a composition, here beautifully balanced by quince blossom and double hyacinths. The other double flowers – peonies, poppies, roses and anemones – float like a mass of silk scarves across the centre of the painting, but the tulips and narcissi of springtime still sing out, and the snakeshead fritillary and honeysuckle still droop.

The new flowers that van Huysum introduced into his paintings were the auriculas (clustered at the lip of the vase and on the ledge). They were bred from alpine flowers the colour of cowslips, until the pale 'paste' at the centre of each flower contrasted with many velvety shades of purple, maroon, brown and green, arousing feverish collectors' instincts reminiscent of what happened with tulips. Among the roses, van Huysum's double yellow *Rosa hemisphaerica* was the latest breed, with Persian genes reluctant to flourish in the damp climate of Dutch gardens. One year van Huysum wrote to the Duke of Mecklenburg, excusing himself for an unfinished painting on the grounds that the yellow rose had not flowered – a rare glimpse of the master's own words, which may explain the false impression that he took years to complete every flower painting.

Flowers in a Vase 1726
Oil on panel, 80 x 60.1 cm
Wallace Collection, London

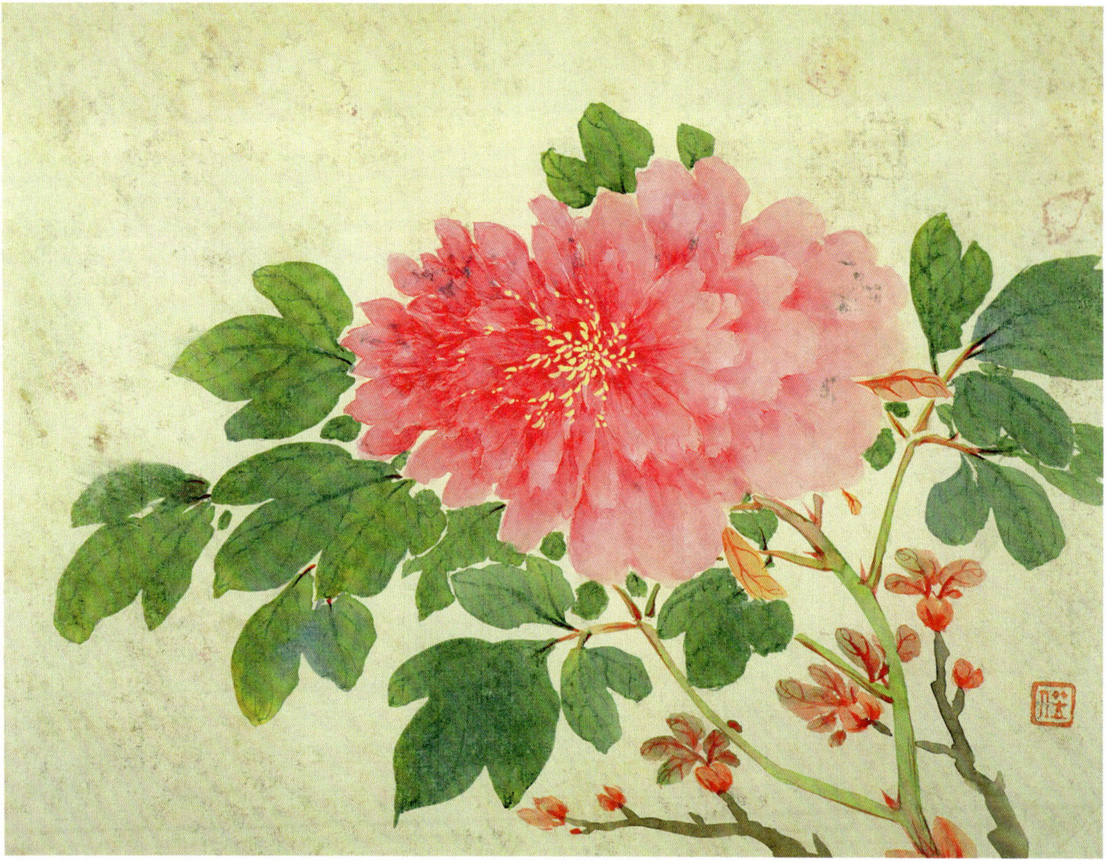

Peonies from *Album of Paintings of Flowers, Fruits, Birds and Animals* c.1774
Watercolour on paper, 20 x 26 cm
School of Oriental and African Studies, University of London

JIANG YU (flourished *c.*1774)

Peony

Peonies from China, which we call tree peonies, did not reach Europe until the 1790s and the early arrivals were always pink, although for centuries the Chinese had been cultivating different colours – passionately searching in the April flower markets for new varieties to place strategically in their garden collections. A Tang dynasty poet writing in the ninth century compared peony flowers to embroidered quilts, concluding with the line, 'I wish to write on petals a message to the clouds of morning'.

For Chinese artists, whose work was designed for scrolls and albums, painting was very close to writing. Similar calligraphic strokes were used in creating their complex words and a child would learn to write with an ink-loaded brush, having to master its versatility to become an educated person. Like ink, an artist's watercolours were not mixed (heavy pigments would have rubbed and cracked when the album was closed or the scroll rolled up). Instead a wide brush was loaded with different strengths of the same pigment, some thinned with water to create the palest wash, whereupon an entire modelled and shaded petal could be produced in one breathtaking stroke. Or one colour could be washed over another while still wet, so they would shine through and modify each other. The innate patterning skills which are the basis of writing were extended to the portrayal of natural things – bamboo and pine were classic examples – and having practised a method for years, and studied the styles of past masters, a Chinese artist did not have to be in front of a landscape or a flower in order to paint it. Instead the moments in a beauty spot or garden would be spent in contemplation and observation, to refresh the spirit – because Chinese religion and philosophy were based on being in harmony with nature – and later in his studio the artist would combine his inspiration and technical expertise, his emotions and his sense of pattern, to express nature. The aim was always realism.

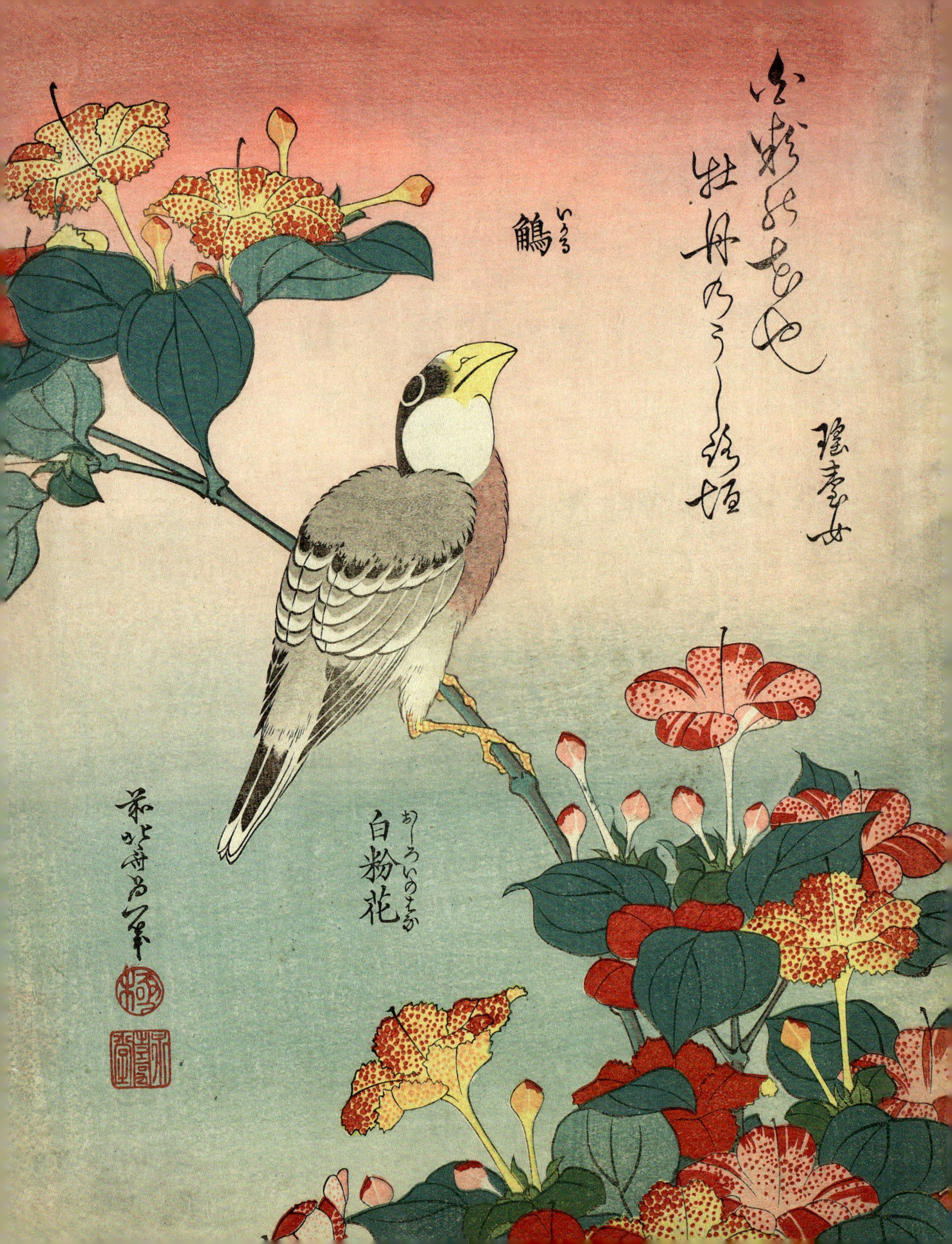

鶍
白粉花
前北斎為一筆

KATSUSHIKA HOKUSAI (1760–1849)

Marvel of Peru (Mirabilis Jalapa)

In the work of Hokusai several traditions met. For centuries Chinese and Japanese artists had created series of watercolour paintings of flowers (with birds and insects) designed for binding in albums. Both countries also developed woodblock printing with colour, and in eighteenth-century Japan the technique was adapted with exquisite finesse to create prints known as Ukiyo-e (The Floating World) where courtesans and actors posed in elaborate costumes, often patterned with emblematic flowers. But of the outstanding Ukiyo-e artists only Hokusai devoted some of his energies to producing series of floral prints in the tradition of album paintings – although in his own boldly innovative style, developed from the harsh discipline of infusing woodblock prints with vitality.

First, however, Hokusai broke with oriental tradition and, adapting elements of perspective he had discovered in European engravings, began producing views of the pleasure districts of Edo (now Tokyo) from unusual angles. In 1793 he was repudiated by the master of the school where he had trained, but his independent career flourished, and he extended his repertoire to celebrated beauty spots – crashing waterfalls, landscapes spanned by bridges and views of Mount Fuji – most famously *The Great Wave* with the mountain glimpsed beyond its foaming curve and a tiny boat struggling in its hollow. Then in the 1830s Hokusai, still at the peak of his career – turning out thousands of prints and surrounded by students – started producing prints of flowers. 'Nothing I did before the age of 70 was worthy of attention', he declared, 'then I began to grasp the way plants grow. If I go on trying I will surely understand them better ... so that by 90 I will have penetrated to their essential nature.' He approached the matter with his particular instinct for line, pattern and colour, and characteristically he chose unusual flowers, not always traditional favourites. The night-flowering Marvel of Peru had been recently introduced into Japan from South America by the Dutch, the only Europeans then allowed to trade with Japan.

Hawkfinch and Marvel of Peru c.1834
Woodblock print, ink and colour on paper, 24.1 x 19 cm
Museum of Fine Art, Boston

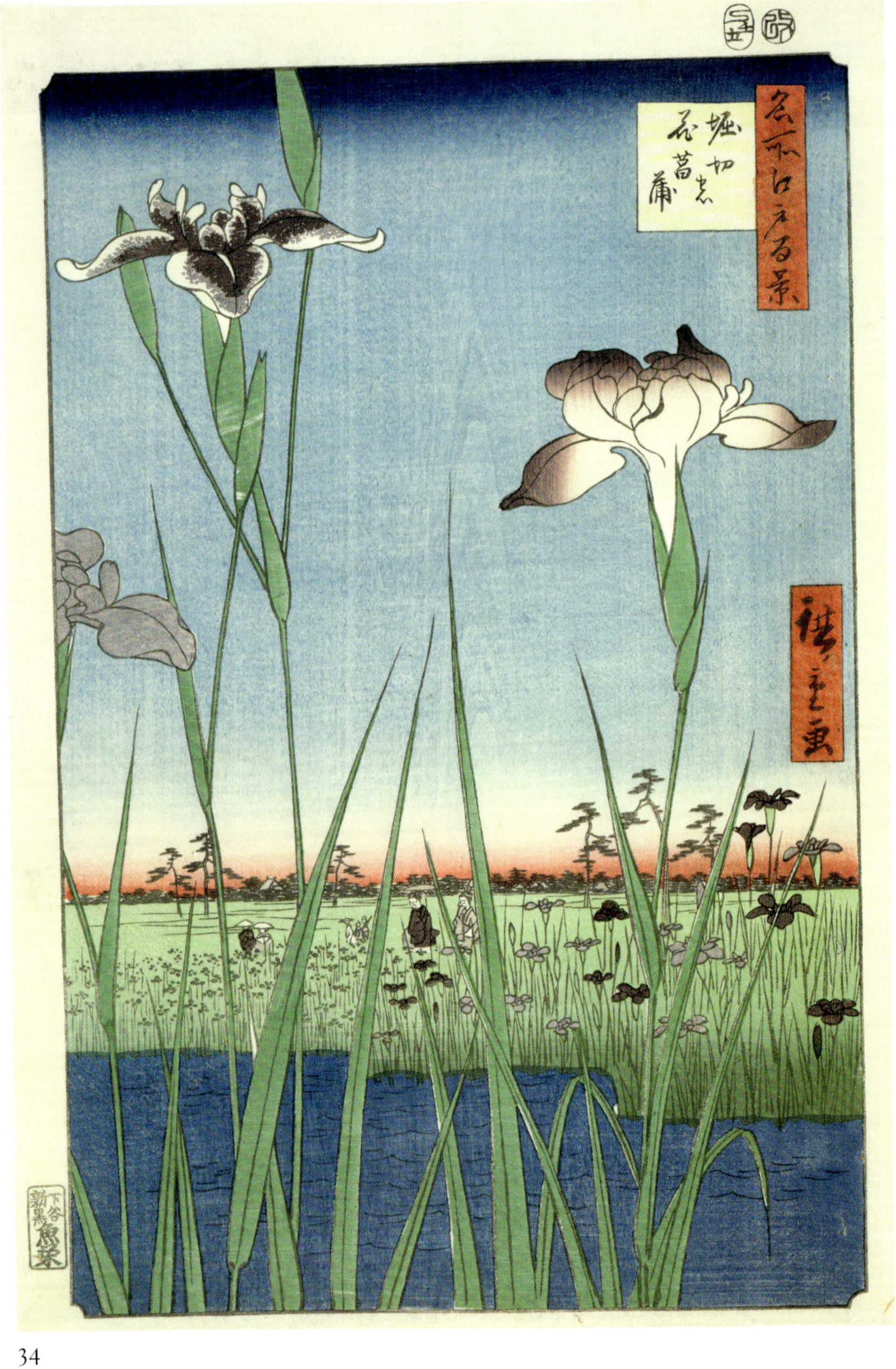
名所江戸百景
堀切の花菖蒲
広重画

UTAGAWA HIROSHIGE (1797–1858)

Irises

Like Hokusai, whom he greatly admired although he did not train with him, Hiroshige began his career with prints of actors and courtesans and in the 1830s made his mark with landscapes. He travelled the 300 mile highway known as the Tokaido from Edo (Tokyo) to Kyoto and published *The Fifty-three Stations* depicting travellers along the famous route in all seasons, including driving diagonal rain and deep snow. In 1857 his final great publication before retiring to become a Buddhist monk was *One Hundred Views of Edo*, not a new subject, but one he transformed into lyrical scenes and energised by using surprising vantage points.

Hiroshige's great flower prints belong in this series of views of Edo. *The Plum Garden at Kameido* (see Introduction) celebrates the springtime picnics among the blossom trees of the capital, with the flowering branches dramatically crossing the foreground; and *The Iris Garden at Horikiri* records the visits made in May to the plant nurseries on the edge of Edo to see the irises in all their glory. Japanese irises (*Iris ensata*) are delicate, spreading flowers, more like parasols than the European species, and they grow in water. Hence the blue stream flowing between the arrestingly close-up flowers in the foreground and the iris plantations beyond, where a few distant enthusiasts wander like rice pickers in a paddy field. The gardeners of Horikiri grew all types of flowers, but they were famous for their irises. Basically Japanese irises are reddish-purple or blue flowers with a yellow blaze on the lower petals, but at Horikiri they had developed pink, lavender and white hybrids, double flowers, and even varieties with bicoloured patterns edging and dividing their petals, as seen here.

In 1853 Japan was forcibly opened to trade by an American fleet, and in the 1870s the nurseries of Horikiri developed a booming export trade in Japanese irises, just as Japanese woodblock prints began arousing enthusiasm and emulation in the West.

One Hundred Views of Edo: The Iris Garden at Horikiri 1857
Colour woodblock print, 39 x 26 cm
Fitzwilliam Museum, University of Cambridge

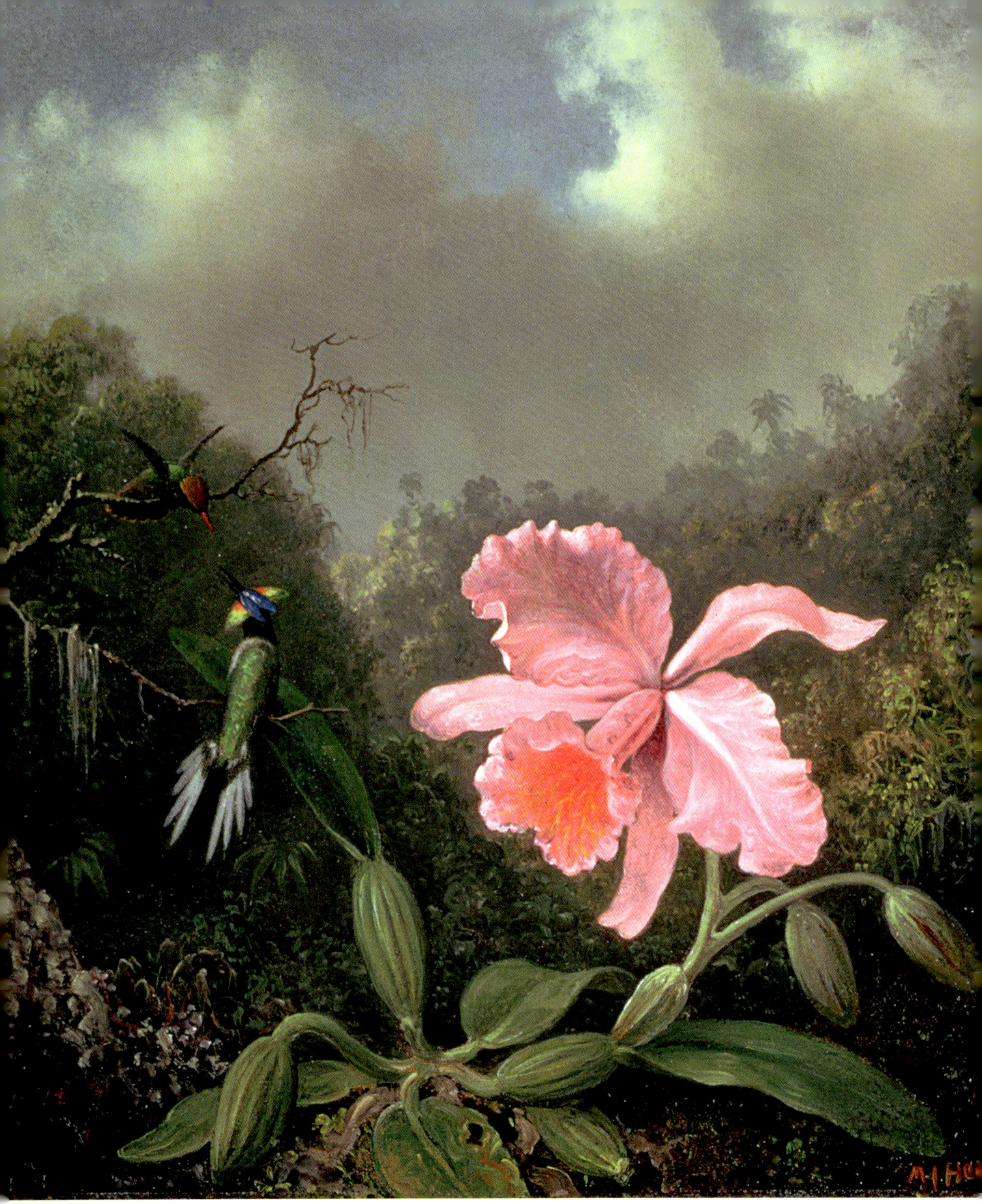

MARTIN JOHNSON HEADE

(1819–1904)

Cattleya

Early in his artistic career Martin Johnson Heade left Pennsylvania and spent two years in Rome, after which he established his reputation as a New York landscape artist, specialising in the coastal salt marshes of New England – including atmospheric masterpieces of sunset and moonlight. But it was when he visited Brazil in 1863–4 that he found the ingredients of his most exciting paintings. His mission was to create an extensive series of humming-bird studies and to make his reputation, like Audubon before him, with a lavish publication. This did not happen, but instead he created many stunning tropical landscapes by using his existing expertise – making distances swoop away into atmospheric mists – then adding the humming birds in action, and dominating the foreground with a massive orchid. Twice more he visited the lands where such orchids grew, Nicaragua in 1866, and in 1870 Colombia, Panama and Jamaica, then in 1883 he moved to Florida. For the rest of his life he used the studies he had made in the rainforests to compile his trademark paintings.

The orchid is a cattleya, the darling of nineteenth-century society. They were collected almost to extinction, grown in hothouses, worn in buttonholes and corsages, and they gave their name to alluring, spicy perfumes. Cattleyas are indigenous to the forested regions of tropical America from Costa Rica to Brazil and this species, *Cattleya labiata*, was the earliest to be found and named in 1821. *Labiata* refers to the lower petal with its frilly margin forming the entrance to a speckled tube (into which insects must be lured to fertilise the flower). The orchid is an epiphyte, meaning it lives on trees, and has pseudobulbs (the swollen base of each leaf) for absorbing humidity and nutrients. Heade captures the plant's attributes like a botanical artist, but he also gives us its supporting mossy branch, the mountainous jungle beyond, the rain-clouds masking intense light, and above all he suggests the thrill of encountering such an orchid in the wild.

Fighting Humming Birds with Pink Orchid c.1875
Oil on canvas, 40.6 x 35.6 cm
Private collection

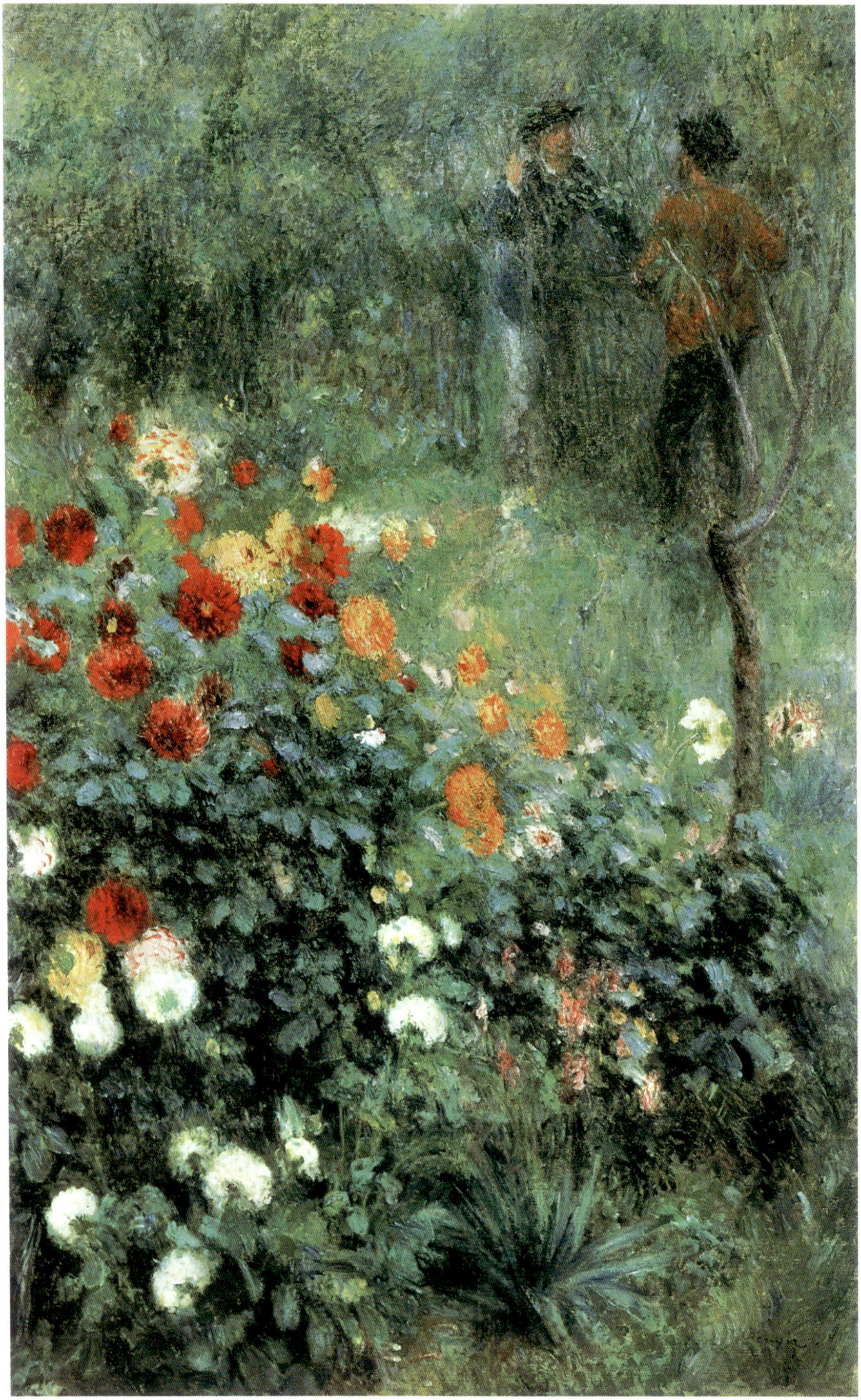

The Garden in the Rue Cortot, Montmartre 1876
Oil on canvas, 152 x 97 cm
Carnegie Museum of Art, Pittsburgh

PIERRE-AUGUSTE RENOIR

(1841–1919)

Dahlias

In the early 1870s Renoir rented a room in the rue Cortot in Montmartre which was part of a dilapidated residence with a rambling garden. Its overgrown delights included neglected orchards, lawns reverted to meadows and rampant flowerbeds. From his window looking downwards Renoir painted this luxuriant swathe of dahlias, gleaming in the filtered sunlight and growing with the carefree abandon that became the hallmark of Impressionist flowers. His loose, feathery brushstrokes recreated their velvety petals, contrasting their rich reds and yellows with the dark blue-green leaves, and setting the white dahlias like lamps to light the green shadows.

At the rustic gate leading to the wooded hills of Montmartre stood Monet and Sisley, chatting and perhaps waiting for Renoir – who painted with the greatest speed and facility because of his initial training decorating porcelain. Three years earlier, in another testament to spontaneity, Renoir had painted Monet in his garden at Argenteuil, standing in front of an easel, brush and palette poised, and painting another bed of dahlias. On the ground lay the box containing the secret of their success, oil paints processed into tubes, a new invention enabling artists to paint outdoors – and more experimentally – instead of labouring in their studios to grind and mix their colours.

In those early years of poverty and lack of recognition, the friendship that kept the Impressionists going is visible in many paintings. Side by side they painted gardens, river scenes, fields of long grass and poppies, and followed Manet into the theatres and bars. Perhaps, beyond the dahlias in the Montmartre garden, Monet and Sisley were waiting for Renoir to come to their favourite rendezvous beside the windmill. Renoir's *Dance at the Moulin de la Galette* was his most famous painting done that year, full of real portraits of the open-air crowd, sparkling with life – like the dahlias – and conveyed by the same technique of thinly brushed, dissolving colours. 'Why', said Renoir, 'shouldn't art be pretty? There are enough unpleasant things in life.'

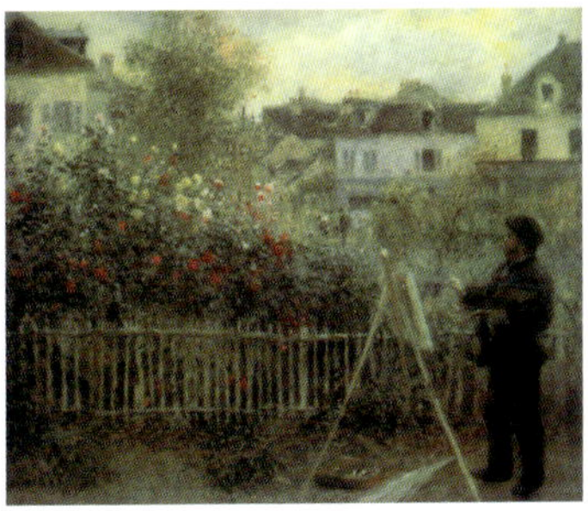

Monet Painting his Garden at Argenteuil 1873
Oil on canvas, 46 x 60 cm
Wadsworth Atheneum Museum of Art, Hartford

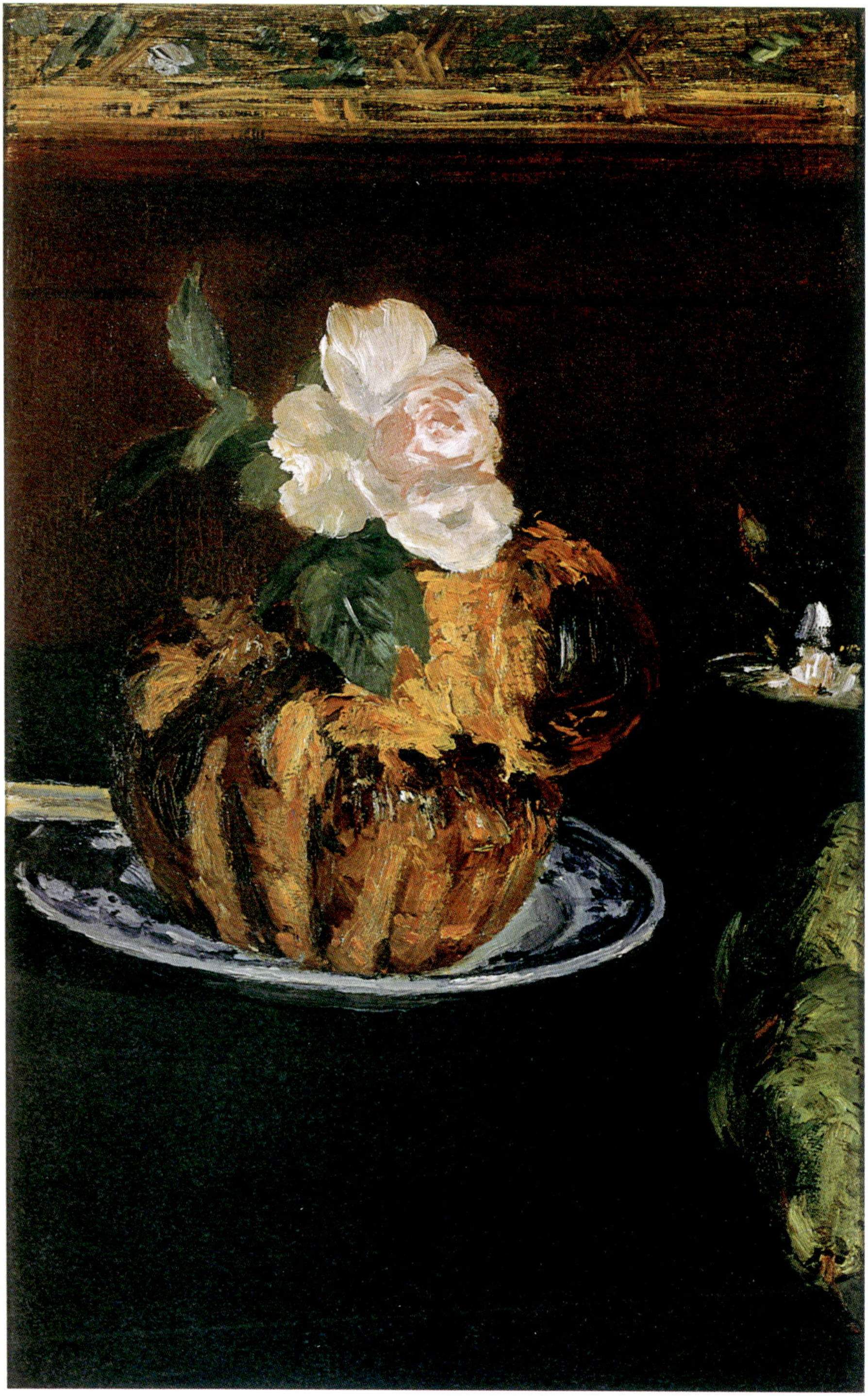

Still Life with Brioche 1880
Oil on canvas,
55 x 35 cm
Carnegie Museum
of Art, Pittsburgh

EDOUARD MANET (1832–83)

Rose

Although he inspired the Impressionists, and drank with them, Manet never considered himself to be one of them. Certainly he was innovative – when he depicted flesh or flowers the looseness of his brushwork endowed them with a mysterious sensuality unseen before – and here the paint on the rose petals is like melting ice cream. But Manet was determined to belong in the mainstream of European art, reinterpreting the achievements of his forebears for his contemporaries. In *Le Déjeuner sur l'Herbe* he quoted Giorgione and Titian who had also painted nude women alongside fully dressed men, and in this still life he paid homage to Chardin, who a hundred years earlier had painted a brioche stuck with a spray of orange blossom. The image is both romantic and puzzling, but originally a flower in a brioche simply indicated its flavour – orange blossom and rose petals both yield scented water used in confectionary – and early still lifes sometimes showed pinks, with their scent of cloves, decorating pastries.

The rose itself is a beauty, its subtle creamy pink much enhanced by the crusty gold tones of the brioche, as if Manet were flaunting his skill at stimulating the senses with paint. Indeed he said that flowers and brioches were both excellent tests of an artist's powers. His painting also records the perfect form of the new hybrid tea rose, first bred in 1867 by the French nurseryman Guillot of Lyons. Its distinguishing features were the outward pointing centre of the flower, the recurved edges of the petals, and an exotic smell of fresh tea leaves, all traceable to oriental ancestry. The traditional roses of Europe flowered all too briefly, and a transformation took place with the introduction of Chinese roses which were capable of flowering repeatedly throughout the summer. By crossing these with the sturdier and more colourful roses of Europe, rose breeders first created the Bourbon rose, then the hybrid perpetuals, and finally the hybrid tea rose, ready for Manet to stick in a brioche and paint.

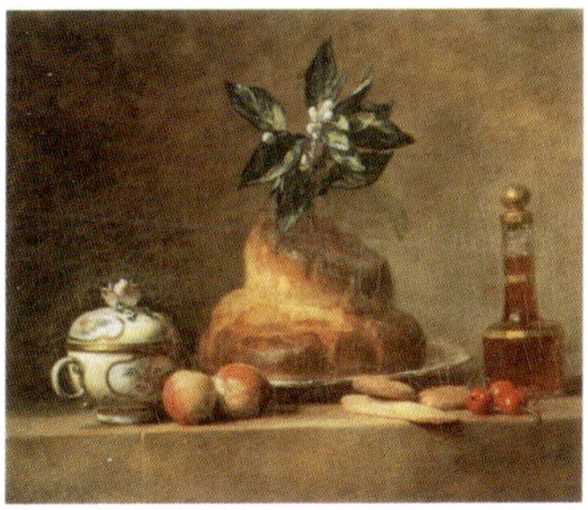

JEAN BAPTISTE SIMEON CHARDIN
Still Life with Brioche 1763
Oil on canvas, 47 x 56 cm
Louvre, Paris

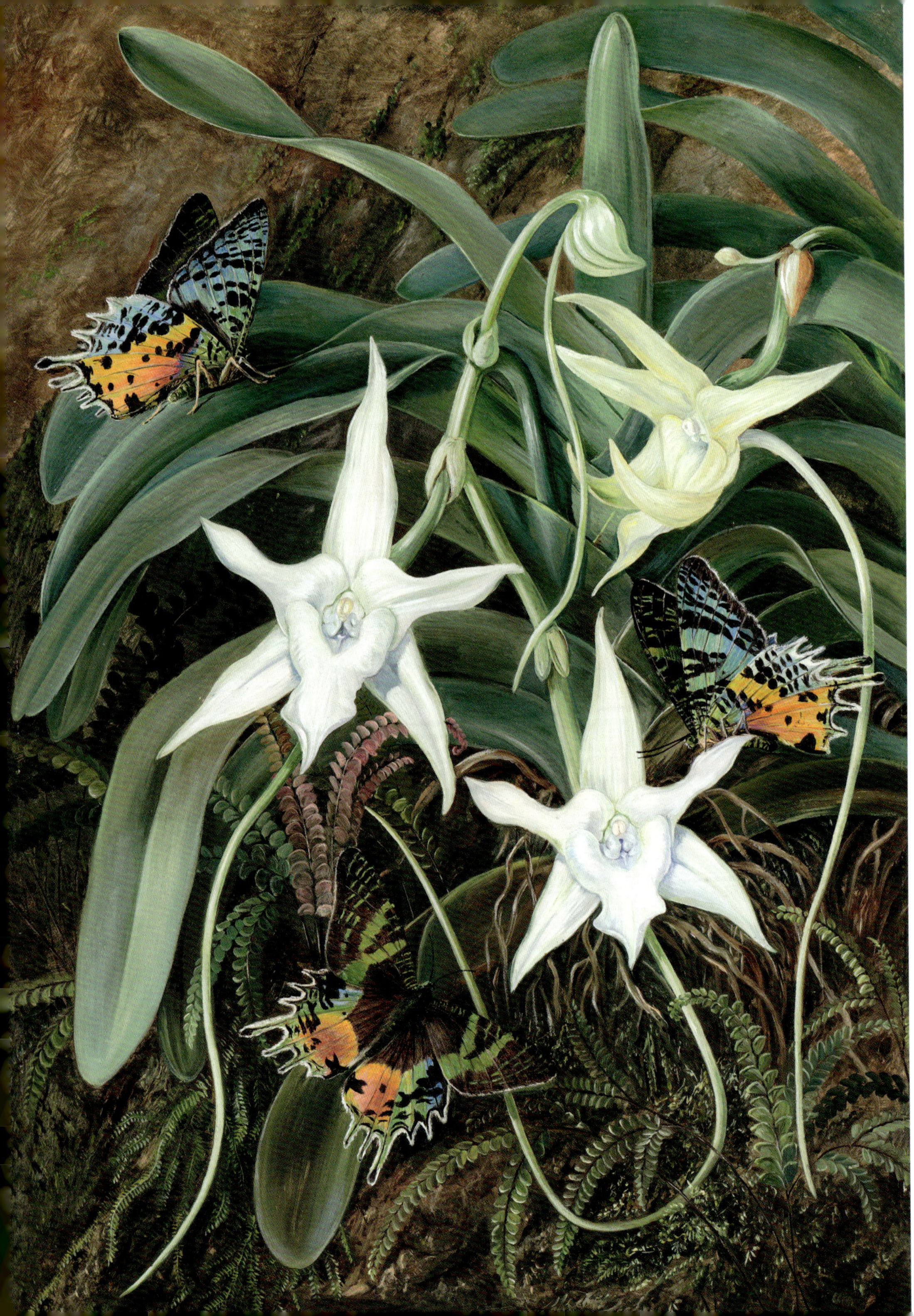

MARIANNE NORTH (1830–90)

Orchid

Until she was forty-one Marianne North lived the pleasant society life of a Victorian lady. She painted and grew orchids, travelled as far as the Mediterranean and had links with the scientific world of Kew Gardens and Charles Darwin. Then in 1871 she began an intrepid series of far-flung expeditions, declaring, 'I had long had the dream of going to some tropical country to paint its peculiar vegetation on the spot'. Eventually her travels included America, India, the East Indies, Australia and South Africa – and sometimes background views of mountains, rivers or temple precincts gave her plants a sense of place.

Orchids inspired more of her paintings than any other flower. Since many of her contemporaries shared this passion, tropical orchids were being collected in increasing quantities to grace the hothouses of Europe. But for Marianne North the thrill was to set off in some perilous boat or wagon, then clamber through jungle tracks where wild orchids dangled from the trees or grew across inaccessible boulders.

By 1879 she had produced over 500 paintings and her old friend Charles Darwin encouraged her to endow a gallery for them at Kew. That same year, while Marianne North was at home, *Angraecum sesquipedale*, one of the most sensational of orchids, arrived at Veitch's plant nursery in Chelsea from Madagascar. Darwin himself was fascinated by the evolutionary adaptations of orchid flowers to be pollinated by specific insects. He had first seen *Angraecum sesquipedale* when he reached Madagascar during the voyage of the *Beagle*, and in 1862 he wrote an article explaining that the amazing white tubes emanating from the flowers contained nectar to attract a moth with a proboscis long enough to unfurl and reach it while simultaneously being dusted with pollen to fertilise the next *Angraecum* flower it visited.

Marianne North visited the Seychelles in 1883, but not Madagascar, and it seems that she painted *Angraecum sesquipedale* in England, though few would realise this because her skill in creating tropical backgrounds had become innate.

Angraecum and Urania Moth of Madagascar 1882–83
Oil on paper, 33 x 46.5 cm
Royal Botanic Gardens, Kew

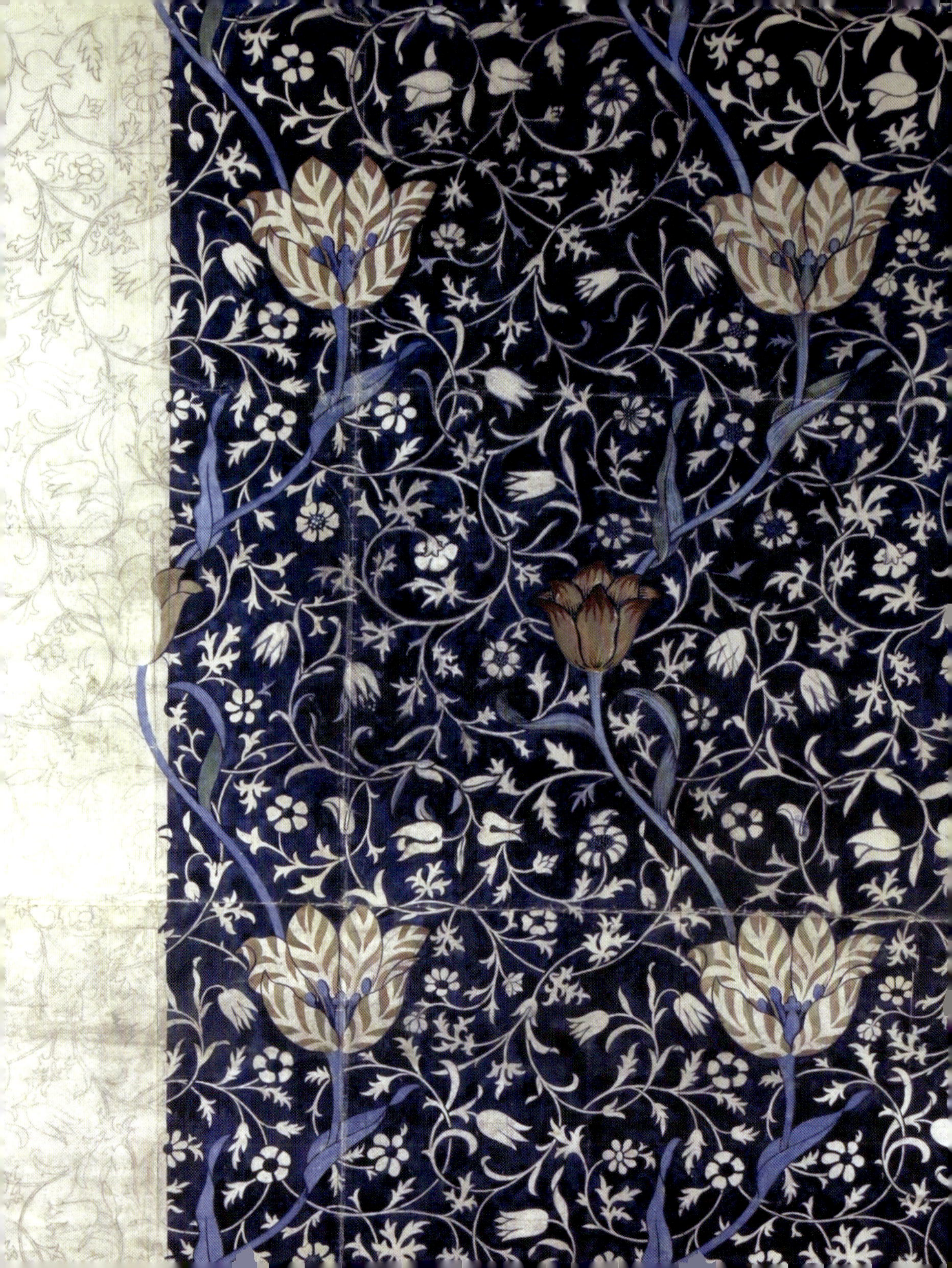

WILLIAM MORRIS (1834–96)

Tulips

The manufacturing firm of Morris and Co. was founded in 1861 and included work by the Pre-Raphaelite artists Rossetti and Burne-Jones. As an ardent socialist William Morris wished to produce art for the masses, but he also insisted on fine and traditional craftsmanship, which meant only the rich could afford his furnishings. Despite these contradictions, he masterminded a thriving business with an iconic style, himself creating the elaborate flowery designs for which he is chiefly famed – the trellis of roses, the sprays of blossom and honeysuckle, and the elaborate confections of many petals based on tulips and chrysanthemums amid swirling acanthus leaves.

William Morris's *Medway* design was part of his river series; most, like *Windrush*, *Cherwell* and *Evenlode*, were tributaries of the Thames and were inspired by a summer boating trip in 1880 from his London home at Hammersmith to Kelmscott Manor in Gloucestershire. The most elaborate river chintz was called *Wandle* after the 'helpful stream' which flowed past the Morris workshops at Merton Abbey. Two others, *Medway* and *Cray*, were Kentish rivers associated with the Red House at Bexleyheath, built by Philip Webb after William and Janey Morris were married in 1859. Here Janey Morris produced the first embroideries designed by Morris, including the much-repeated Daisy design, which she worked in wool on an indigo fabric.

Janey's blue background was used again for *Medway* with a delicate design of arabesques sprouting tiny tulips and anemones. The 'wavy stem' motif linking the larger flowers derived from Islamic brocades, where it designated the water channels of a garden. Morris was fascinated by oriental influences and appreciated this connection with his rivers. In *Wandle* the curving lines did look more like water rills, but in *Medway* they reverted to 'wavy stems' with leaves. The red tulips in Medway were reminiscent of the tulips in Morris tapestries (where they had a medieval look) and by contrast the larger tulips with pale, stylised stripes looked excitingly innovative, like harbingers of Art Nouveau.

Medway, tulip design 1885
Pencil and watercolour on paper, 129.5 x 101.5 cm
William Morris Gallery, London Borough of Waltham Forest

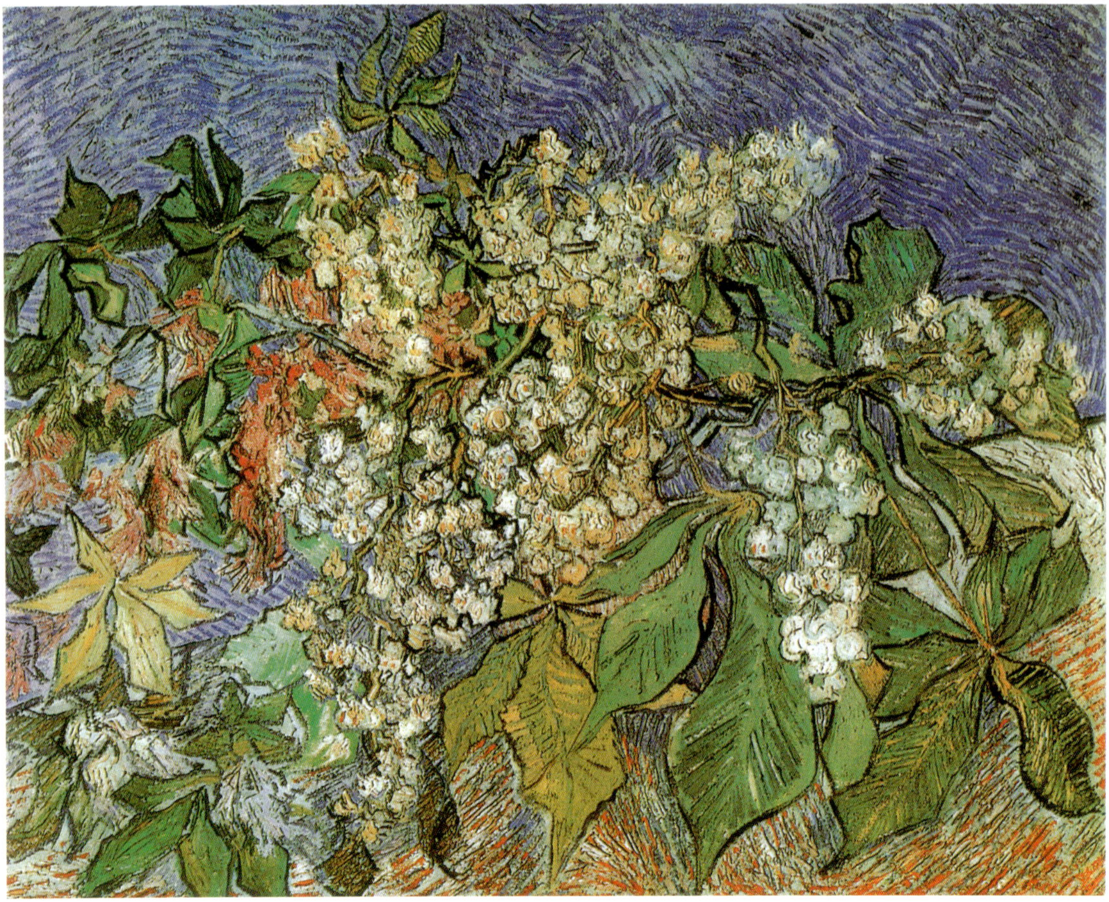

Blossoming Chestnut Branches 1890
Oil on canvas, 72.5 x 91 cm
Bührle Collection, Zurich

VINCENT VAN GOGH (1853–90)

Chestnut blossom

When Van Gogh first turned from religion to art to expel his demons he painted dark interiors and poverty, but arriving among the Impressionists in Paris in 1886 colour became his obsession. In the letters which he produced as frenetically as his paintings he described his search for contrasts, often in terms of flowers: 'Cornflowers and marigolds – motif in blue and orange; poppies or geraniums in vigorous green leaves – motif in red and green'. Or, more disturbingly, 'I have tried to express with red and green the terrible passions of human nature'. Among the cottage gardens of Montmartre, he started on sunflowers, first on a blue ground, then red, then against a flurry of flickering blue, red and green brushstrokes. In Arles in 1888, where he intended to 'get up enough heat to melt the gold', he tried other backgrounds for his sunflowers, 'from palest malachite' to royal blue and, most famously, yellow itself against which the 'broken chrome yellows blaze forth'.

But Van Gogh arrived in Arles while it was still winter, and the first flowers he painted were the white and pink blossoms of the fruit trees as they unfolded against a suddenly brilliant blue sky. He also made wonderful drawings of the trees themselves – both wild and calligraphic – done quickly with a goose quill. So it was among the blossom trees of Arles that he finally moved his painting into the open and used the sky itself as his background.

After his breakdown in Arles, Van Gogh returned early in 1890 to his long-suffering brother Theo in Paris, who put him under the care of Dr Gachet in Anvers, hoping his expertise and the countryside would bring peace of mind. Once more springtime seized Vincent. Those last months of frantic painting began in May, with the chestnuts, and ended in July with his death. The horror of it is in the sky pulsing with blue lines, but so is the vigorous assertion of life, the truth to nature, the reds and greens, and the creamy blossoms harmonising the extremes.

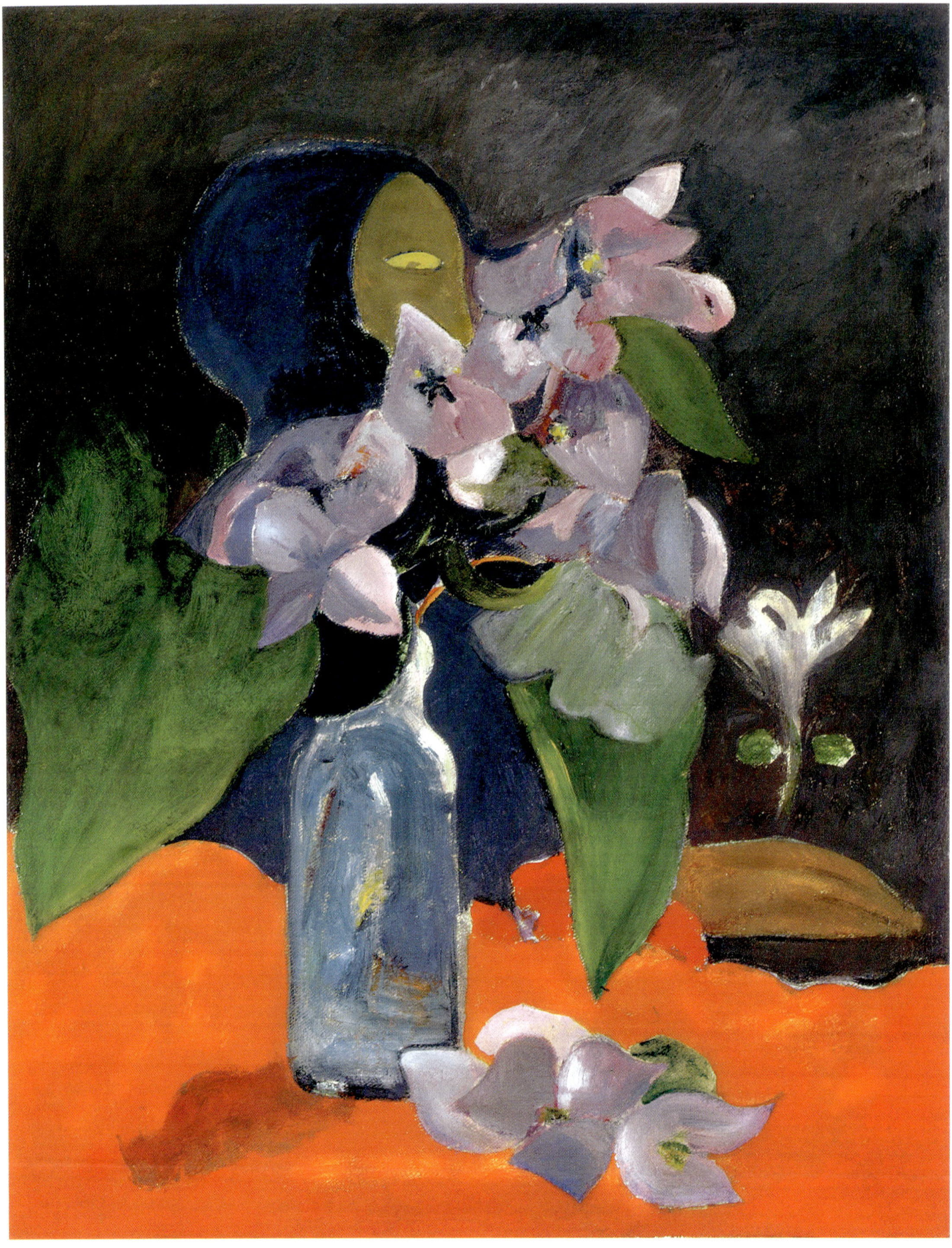

PAUL GAUGUIN (1848–1903)

Bougainvillea

During the decade before he left for Tahiti in 1891 Gauguin gave up his comfortable family life as a Paris stockbroker who collected Impressionist paintings to become an artist himself; no longer seeking to capture the reality before his eyes, as his mentors did, but something more elemental. He sought inspiration in the primitive arts of ancient civilisations, modelling ceramic heads (including his own) with powerful crudity, and he claimed his own blood was savage (his mother's people were Spanish colonists in Peru). Gauguin first went on record with the term Symbolist in 1887, seeking to explain his simplified compositions, with their emphatic, rhythmic outlines and areas of unnatural, saturated colour.

The colours in this still life are as vibrant, dark and flowing as only Gauguin's could be. Against them the soft, pale mauves and shadows of the bougainvillea flowers are subtle and evoke tenderness. But the tropical green leaves look poisonous, and the beautiful lake of red is the scarlet of fresh blood. Above the red rests the hand of the idol, and its hooded head lurks in the darkness behind the flowers. During that first year in Tahiti Gauguin painted the same idol's sinister profile in *The Spirit of the Dead Keep Watch*, with the terrified girl lying face down on her bed. It appeared again in preparatory studies for *Words of the Devil*, although in the finished painting the idol became a kneeling witchdoctor chanting behind a mass of red flowers as the uneasy girl clutched a cloth to her groin.

These watching eyes were always yellow, a colour slightly reflected in the centres of the bougainvillea flowers, seeming to mar their innocence and beauty. Often Gauguin's still lifes included meaningful images: on the wall behind a vase of peonies, a full-skirted Degas ballerina; a Delacroix sketch of Adam and Eve, behind a bowl of tropical fruit; a Japanese print of a Kabuki actor playing a distraught ghost, behind flowers where Gauguin's own ceramic profile formed the vase. Are the greatest flower paintings expressions of the artist's own emotions?

Still Life with Flowers 1892
Oil on canvas, 40.5 x 32 cm
Kunsthaus, Zurich

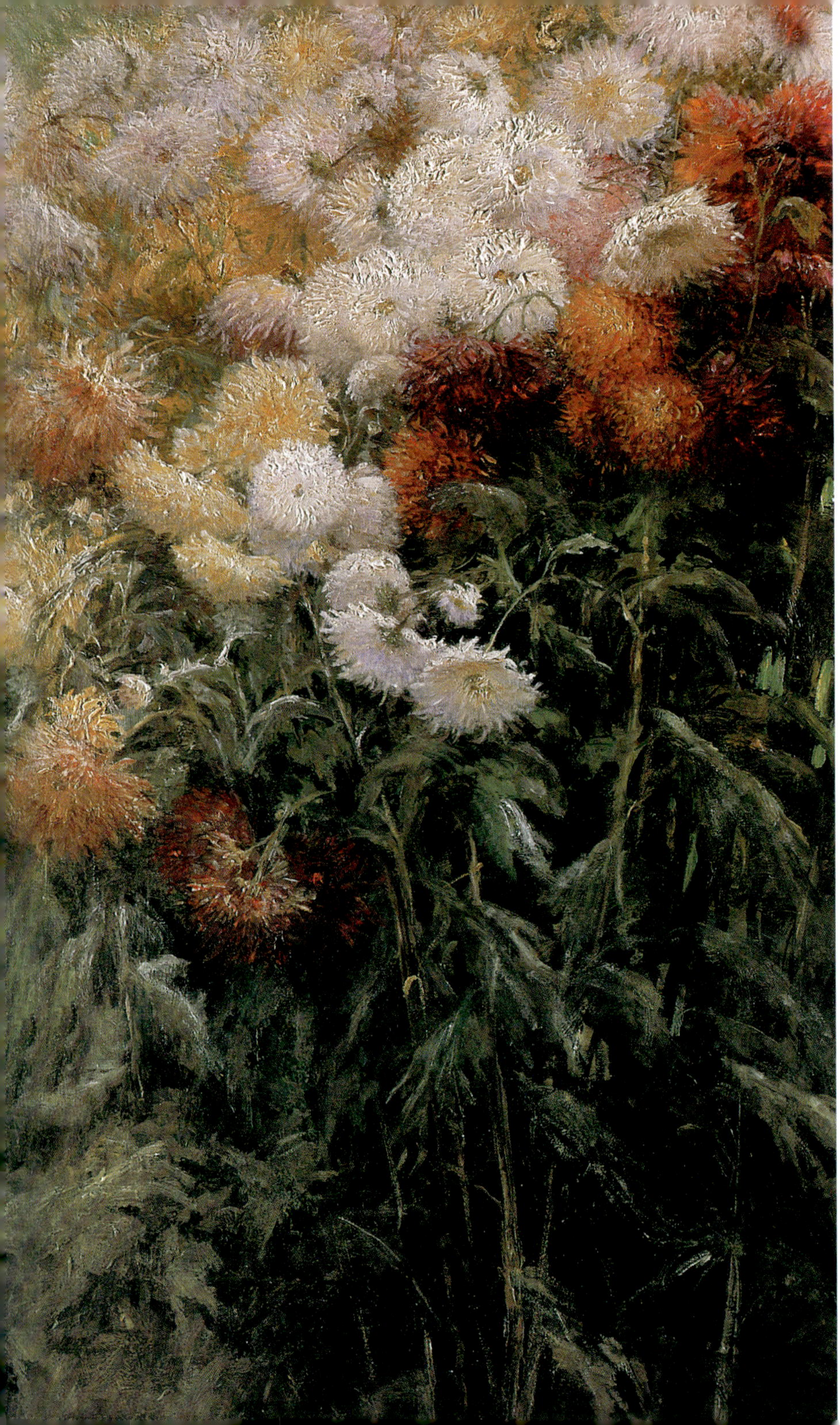

Clump of Chrysanthemums, Garden at Petit Gennevilliers 1893
Oil on canvas,
99 x 61.3 cm
Private collection

GUSTAVE CAILLEBOTTE (1848–94)

Chrysanthemums

Caillebotte joined the Impressionist circle after returning from the Franco-Prussian War and inheriting his father's wealth. He helped to organise the first Impressionist exhibition of 1874 (when Monet's painting *Impression sunrise* caused the critics to give them this insulting label). His own paintings were included in all subsequent Impressionist exhibitions, which he largely financed, and in 1877 Emile Zola wrote, 'when his talent has softened a little he will be one of the boldest of the group'. From his friends Monet, Renoir, Degas and Pissarro he bought many paintings at inflated prices and subsequently left them to the unappreciative French nation, although eventually some formed the basis of the collection now in the Musée d'Orsay.

Caillebotte was a man of great ability and enthusiasms. Trained in engineering, he designed, built and raced yachts – and painted boating scenes. The newly invented techniques of photography fascinated him, and many of his paintings have that smooth, glossy surface and include figures gazing from a balcony, or in a garden, as if they have been captured unawares during a fleeting moment. Both photography and the vogue for Japanese prints inspired Caillebotte to experiment with perspective angles and shadows, whether in views over the Paris rooftops or contrasting the purple shadows and intense sunlight on a garden terrace. He often painted scenes from the Caillebotte family property at Yerres, south of Paris on the Seine, but in 1881 he bought his own riverside home at Petit Gennevilliers, and gardening became another passion. When Monet moved to Giverny the two artists corresponded about plants. Caillebotte had hothouses where he collected orchids, and he decorated the doors of his dining room with orchid paintings. With flowers Caillebotte's brushwork softened, growing more Impressionistic, and especially reminiscent of Renoir, who often came to stay.

Here, zooming like a camera lens towards his bed of chrysanthemums, Caillebotte has lovingly conveyed their silky petals, autumnal colours and untidy leaves. He has also created a unique viewpoint for enjoying them.

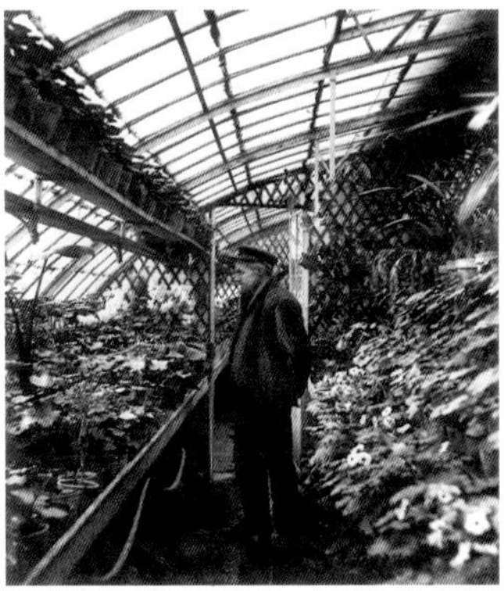

Gustave Caillebotte in his hothouse
Photographic print

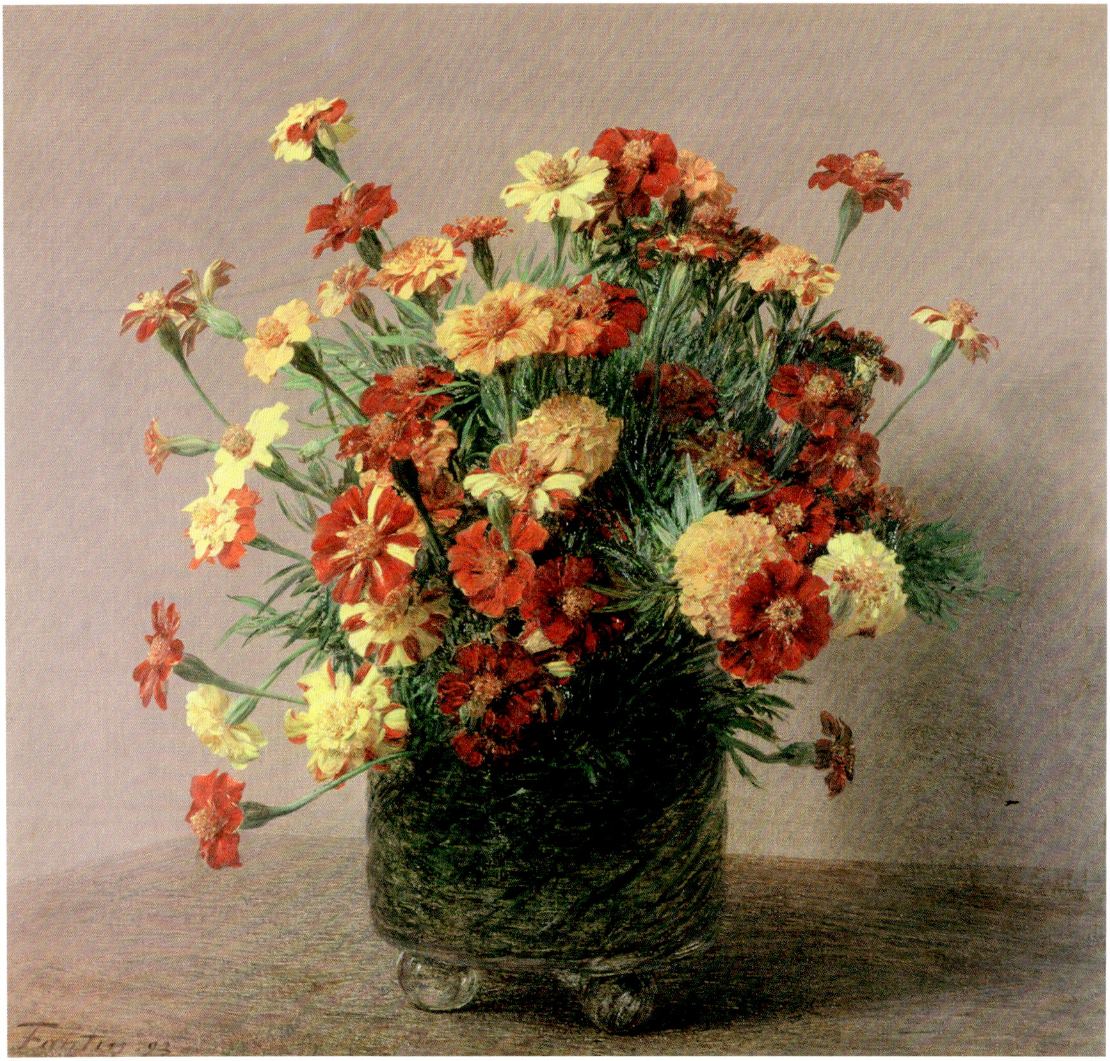

Oeillets d'Inde 1893
Oil on canvas, 46.2 x 49.7
Private collection

HENRI FANTIN-LATOUR (1836–1904)

French marigolds

Henri Fantin-Latour was best loved for his luxuriant paintings of roses, and other high-society bouquets of his time containing delphiniums, dahlias and gladioli. They evoke nineteenth-century drawing rooms and cultured conversation in the style of Proust, thus: 'He asked her whether she had seen the flower painting by Fantin-Latour which had recently been exhibited'.

But Fantin-Latour could also capture more wayward charms, like these French marigolds, stuffed in a glass vase, their yellow, orange and chocolate brown crowded in happy confusion. The blending of their vivid colours and patterns with a hazy pink background (subtly darkening to indicate the table) suggests that by this stage in his career Fantin-Latour was influenced by his more avant-garde contemporaries. His ubiquitous position in the art world was best expressed by his two important group paintings – *Homage to Delacroix* (1864) in which Baudelaire, Manet and Whistler admire the artist's portrait, and *A Studio at Les Batignolles* (1870) showing Monet, Renoir and Emile Zola together in Manet's studio. In 1863 Fantin-Latour even joined his friends in the *Salon des Refusés*, where those who had been rejected by the art establishment displayed their work. However he remained a traditionalist, painting his flowers with delicate precision, and once Whistler had introduced his work across the Channel his paintings were eagerly gathered into English collections.

In England *Tagetes patula* were called French marigolds, probably because they were first introduced by Huguenots fleeing the Catholic repression in France, which culminated in the Massacre of St Bartholomew in 1572. This was not their only association with death, since in their native Mexico tagetes have always been gathered for the Day of the Dead, the graveside celebrations equivalent to Hallowe'en. Like the larger tagetes (also Mexican but known as African marigolds), their various names belie their origins. Fantin-Latour knew them as *oeillets d'Inde*, referring to the West Indies, but recalling Columbus's original confusion in sailing westwards and believing he had almost reached India.

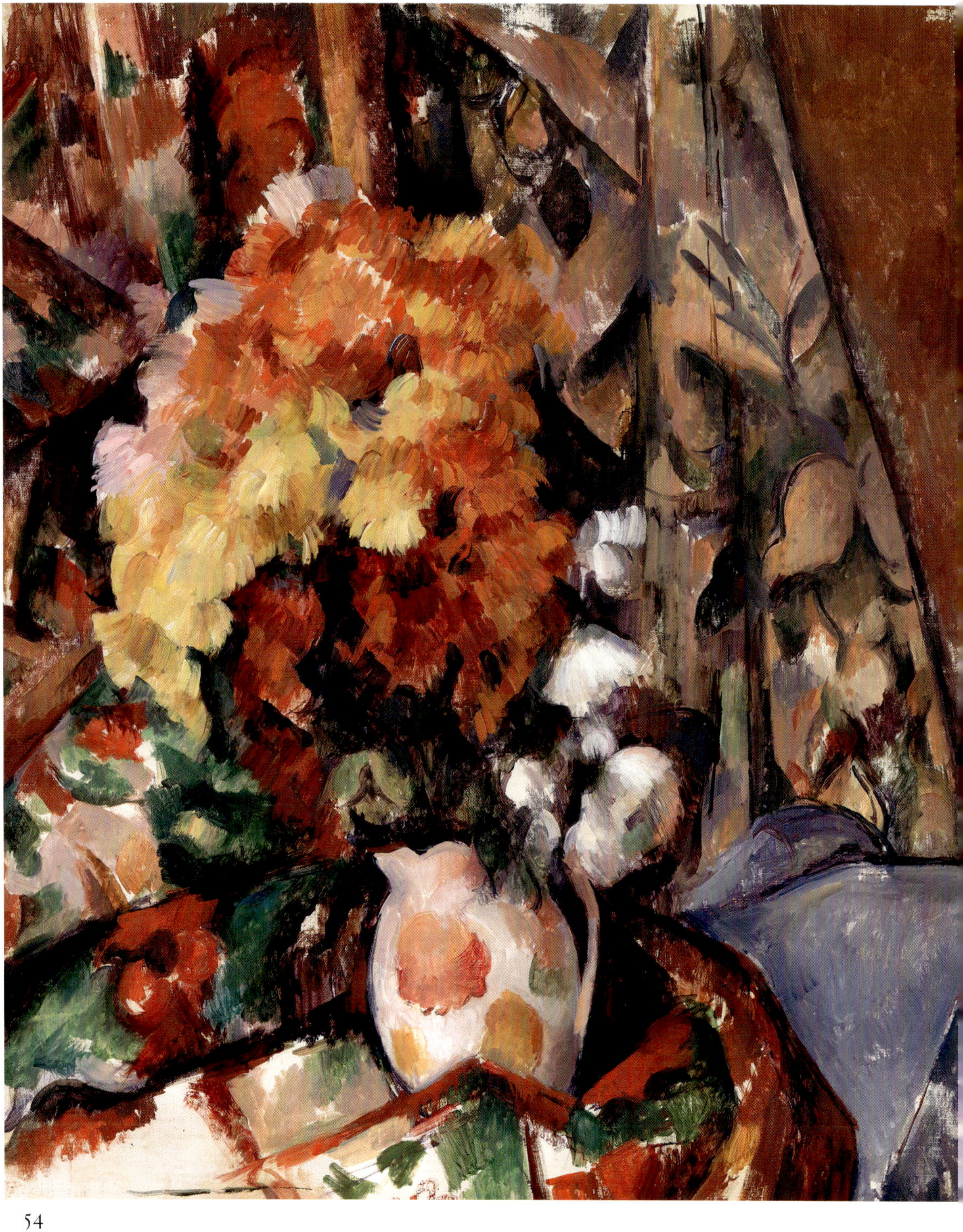

PAUL CEZANNE (1839–1906)

Chrysanthemums

The most astonishing thing in this astonishing painting is that the flowers are undoubtedly chrysanthemums. The short vigorous strokes with which Cézanne has formed their petals prefigure abstract art but, within the context he has created around them, they grow full and silky. They are as innumerable, straight and tufted – and as orange, yellow, red, white and pink – as only chrysanthemums could be, and the staccato brushstrokes make them pulse with energy.

Cézanne arrived in Paris in the 1860s and joined the Impressionists uneasily. Although he shared many of their beliefs about abandoning traditional methods, he loathed their theoretical arguments when they assembled noisily at the Café Guerbois. When painting, he lacked their lightness of touch, and although he believed as fervently as anyone in depicting nature, he needed a process of prolonged and painful concentration to do so. His old school friend Emile Zola thought he might he unhinged by the process, 'the least obstacle makes him despair', and at the first Impressionist exhibition in 1874 a critic picked him out as 'a bit of a madman'. Pissarro with fatherly patience and humour took him to paint trees, and when Cézanne's own rich and autocratic father died in 1886 he retreated to the family estate in Aix. There he concentrated on the landscape of Provence, sunshine bathed his work, and he mastered form in new ways, reworking the rules of shading and recession as this painting clearly shows.

The chrysanthemums have no outlines, but consist of vivid colour and diagonal brushstrokes. The space around them is tilted forwards and is built up in blocks of tone. The background melts away only because the colours of the flowers are reflected by softer or darker washes in the fabrics and the rosy-brown wall. This intense concentration is enhanced by the contrasting blue fabric (Cézanne's trademark faded indigo), and by light shining through the china jug, the brighter chrysanthemums and the white ground of the canvas left unpainted in the lower corner. Such complexities inspired many further experiments from Cubists to Colourists.

The Flowered Vase 1896–98
Oil on canvas, 70.5 x 58.4 cm
The Barnes Foundation, Philadelphia

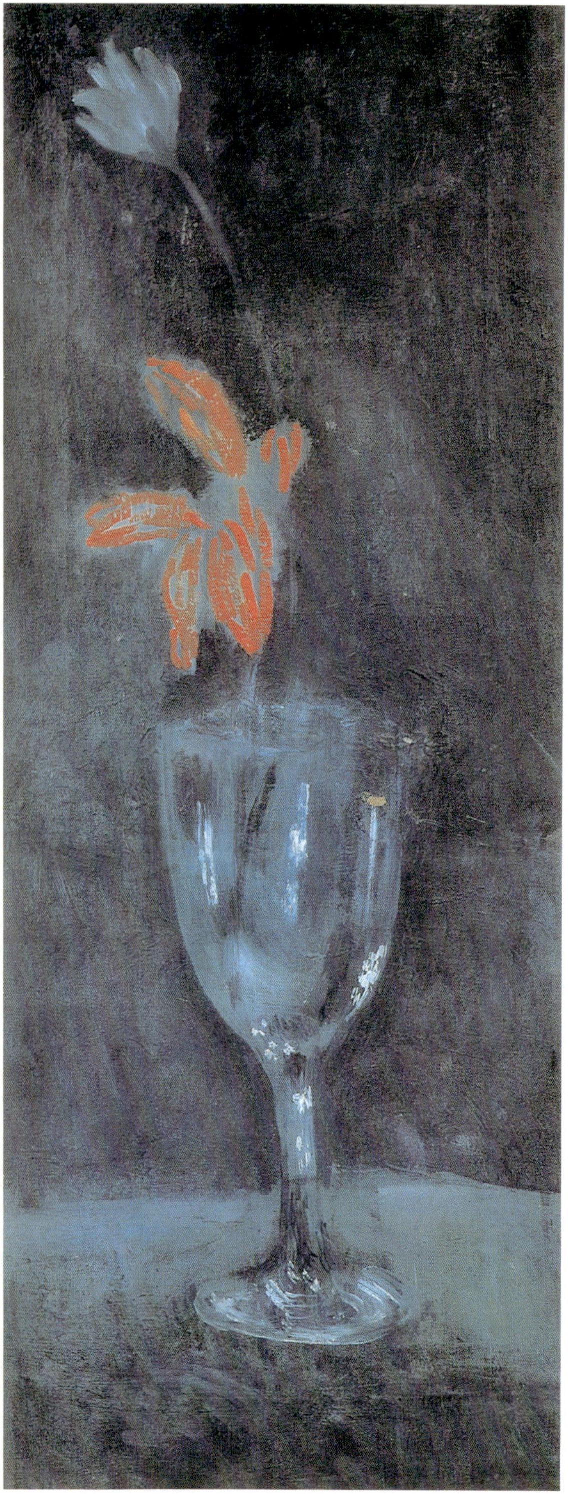

The Blue Glass 1903
Oil on canvas, 66.1 x 28.5 cm
Museu Picasso, Barcelona

PABLO PICASSO (1881–1973)

Dahlia

Picasso's Blue Period lasted from 1901 to 1904, during which time he was still moving between Paris and the family home in Barcelona, before finally settling in France. His subjects were impoverished outcasts, blind, crouched, drunk or starving, but their angular bodies and melancholy faces gave them an allegorical power, much enhanced by the shades of blue in which the works were drenched and the echoes of great masters, especially El Greco, in their haunted eyes and elongated limbs. Degas and Toulouse-Lautrec had already moved art into bars and brothels; the Symbolists also regarded blue as the colour of desolation (or the inspiration may have been an exhibition in Paris of Edward Burne-Jones's blue paintings); but Picasso himself attributed his Blue Period to the suicide of a friend – whom he painted repeatedly over those years – 'I started painting in blue when I learned of Casagemas's death'.

The subject of this painting is the glass, like the absinthe glasses in front of various gaunt figures in other Picasso paintings. The pervasive blue makes the orange flower startlingly vibrant, but whether with the warmth of life or a dangerous flame of intoxication is uncertain given the context of the Blue Period. The flower is a dahlia, not the enlarged bloom of cultivation but closer to the wild flowers of Mexico – and those introduced to Spain during the seventeenth century – which had graceful elongated stalks, like the one that holds the bud above the flower in the blue glass.

Picasso seldom painted flowers, but the colour of the dahlia may have been significant. During 1904, as he moved from Blue Period to Rose Period, warm pinks and oranges touched his figures, which turned from beggars into harlequins, dancers and acrobats. In 1905 he started his affair with Fernande Olivier, won the patronage of Gertrude Stein, met Matisse, and late that year painted the famous *Boy with a Pipe*, with a background of rosy flowers. Perhaps the elegant little orange dahlia was indeed the first glow of warmth in the Blue Period.

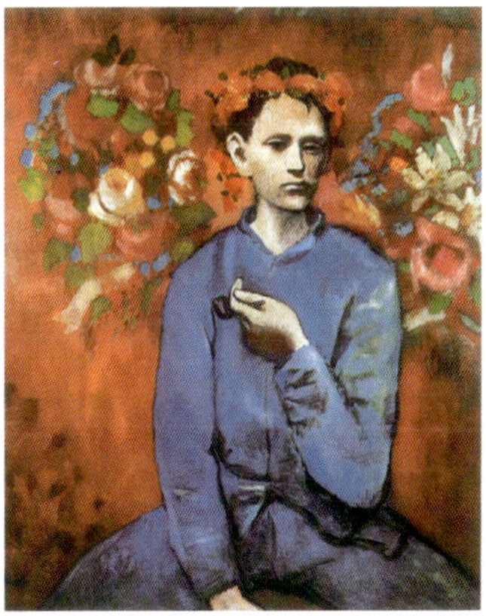

Boy with a Pipe 1905
Oil on canvas, 100 x 81.3cm
Private collection

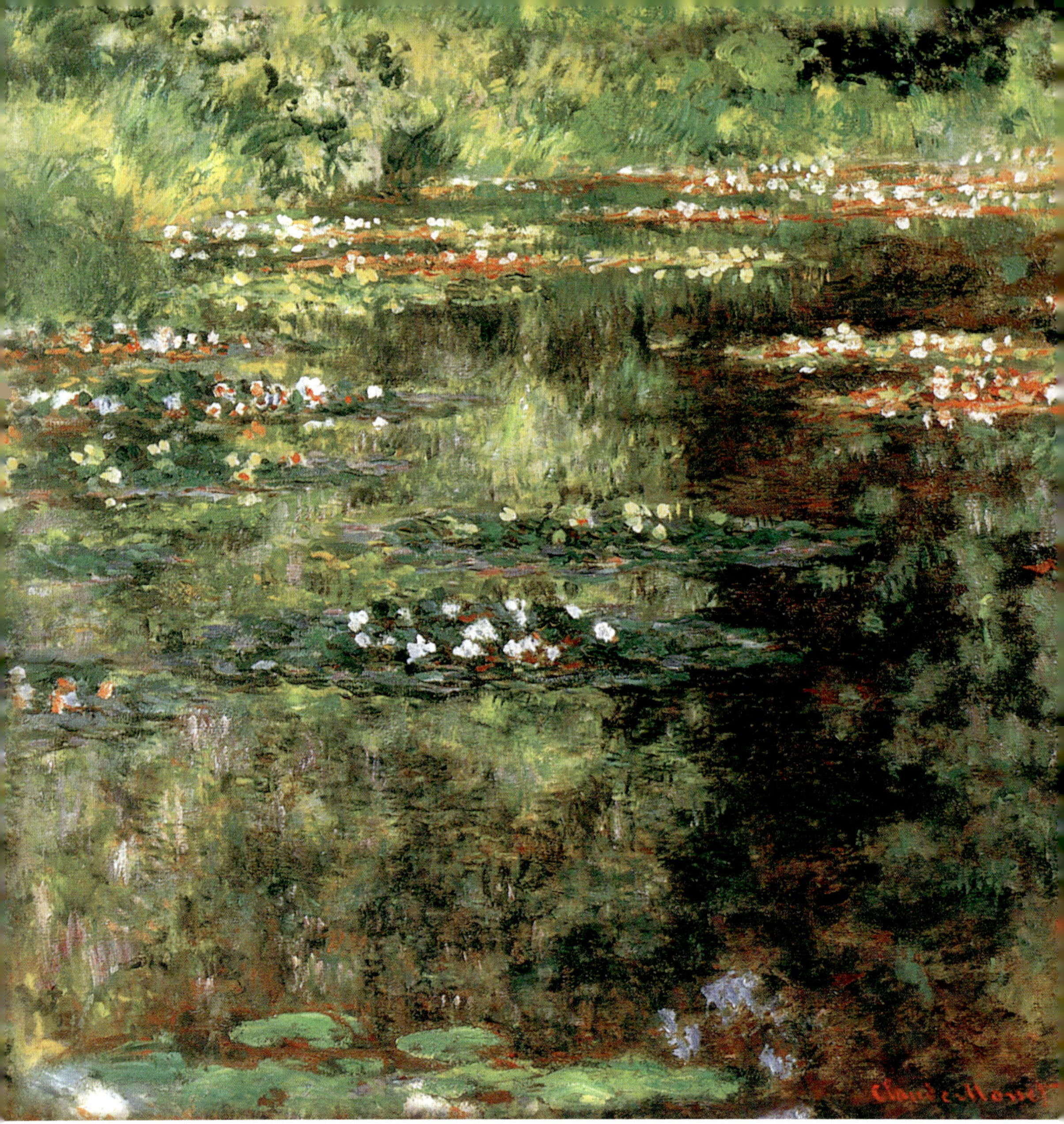

The Water Lily Pond 1904
Oil on canvas, 90 x 92 cm
Private collection

CLAUDE MONET (1840–1926)

Water lilies

In 1893 Monet purchased a meadow beside his garden at Giverny, past which ran a tributary of the River Epte, and embarked on a 'dream long cherished' to create a water garden. The locals opposed him, fearing he would disrupt their water supplies and that his exotic plants would escape to choke the river.

The water lilies did not have disastrous habits, but they were new creations. The plant breeder Bory Latour-Marliac pioneered a method of hybridising wild water lilies (which are white or yellow) to create plants more akin to a lotus. His methods remain secret, but in 1879 he produced *Nymphaea marliacea* in shades of pink, and the yellows followed in 1880. Monet had always been fascinated with juxtaposing the compact brilliance of flowers with the eddying reflections of water. As he put it, 'I love water and I love flowers – I took a catalogue and made the choice – that's all'.

The first exploratory painting of the new water garden dates from 1895, but he wrote years later, 'It took me a long time to understand my water lilies'. In 1898 he had a bonfire of unfinished paintings. Then in 1899 he painted the series spanned by the Japanese bridge, where already he had dispensed with the sky to concentrate on reflections, from the fresh greens of morning to a treacly sunset. In the winters of 1900 and 1901 he was in London in search of fog to maximise the atmosphere of Westminster and the Thames. The following summer, back in Giverny, he purchased another meadow beyond the river to triple the area of his water garden, and ordered more water lilies in the newest vibrant colours – red, copper and turquoise. After this his paintings became a shimmering glance across the water, with the lily pads suspended between heaven and the depths, suggesting the mirroring surface and its constant subtle changes. Their long-awaited exhibition in 1909 was entitled *Water Lilies; Landscapes of Water.*

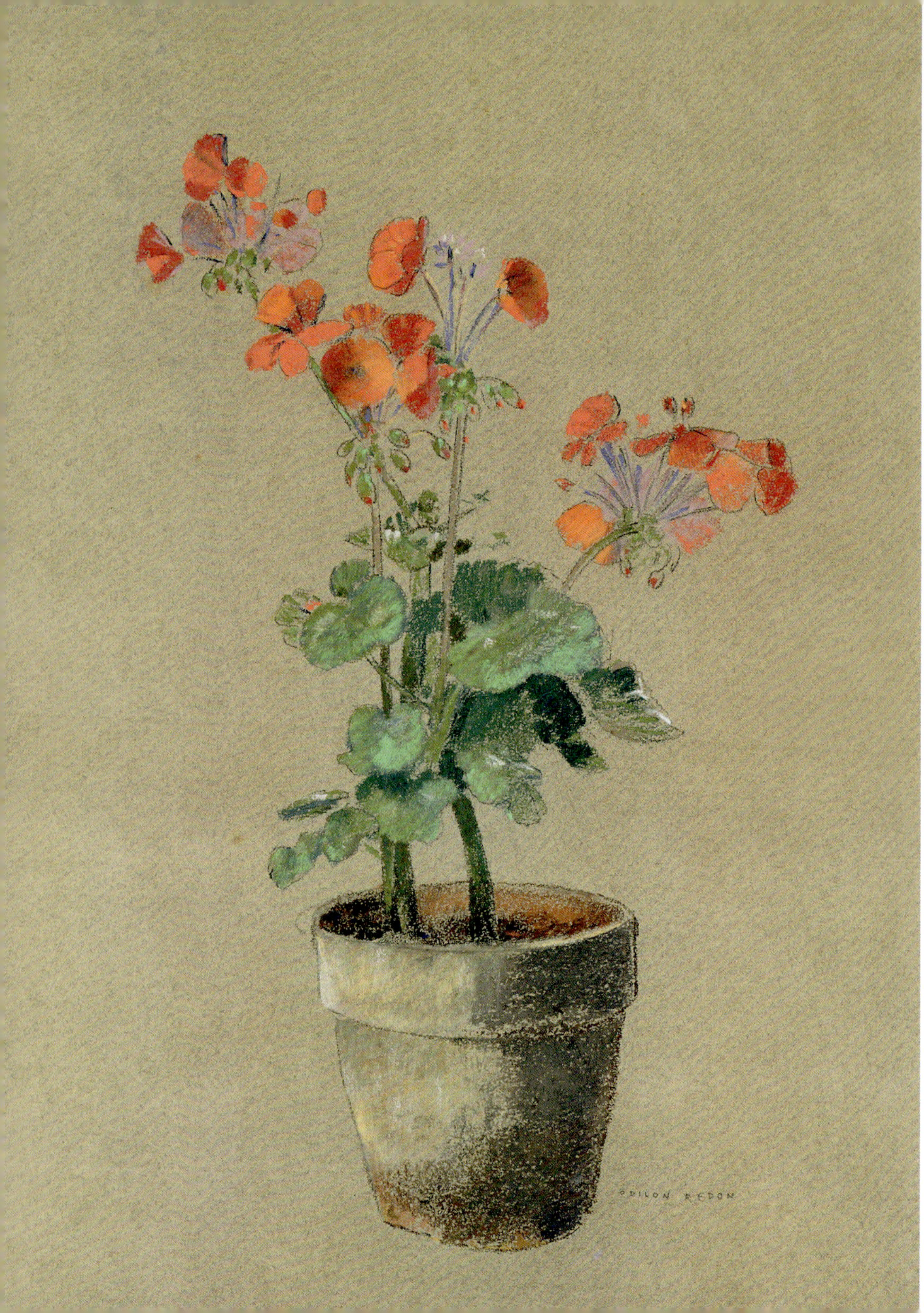
ODILON REDON

ODILON REDON (1840–1916)

Geraniums

This pot of geraniums dates from Odilon Redon's serene old age. The art which made him famous arose from his bleak youth and troubled psyche, much influenced by Baudelaire and Edgar Alan Poe, and manifesting itself in grim lithographs and grey charcoals which he called '*les noirs*' (the blacks). These featured monstrous creatures, and plants with human heads, and were first published in 1879 as *Dans le Rêve* (In the Dream). In 1884 a secret collection of Redon's 'charcoal sketches that delved deep into the terrors of fever-dreams', where 'monstrous flora bloomed on the rocks', was described in the cult novel by Huysmans *A Rebours* (Against Nature). After this Redon gained serious attention and his weird subjects were accepted as – in his own words – 'placing the visible at the service of the invisible'.

Then in the 1890s Redon discovered an astonishing gift for colour, which he expressed with both pastels and oils. Flowers blossomed, especially poppies and anemones, although many of his other blooms remained unreal, and floated in a slightly sinister light, retaining the dreamlike mystery which had made Redon famous. 'Flowers', he wrote, 'have come to the confluence of two streams, that of representation and that of memory'. Redon was recognised as an important influence both by the Surrealists and by the Symbolists (those who believed in the emotional use of colour and distortion, including Bonnard and Matisse). Matisse was a great admirer and bought two of Redon's pastels in 1900.

As for this exquisite pastel of geraniums, without Redon's experience of depicting dreams they would look less real. The floating quality of the scarlet petals makes them seem tangible, and the unnatural blue lines in the little flower stalks emphasise their spikiness. The terracotta pot would not seem so worn and earthy without the skill Redon derived from using charcoals. And without the central green of the leaves the reddish colours would not come to life and sing out as they do.

Geraniums in a Pot 1905
Pastel on paper
Gemeentemuseum, The Hague

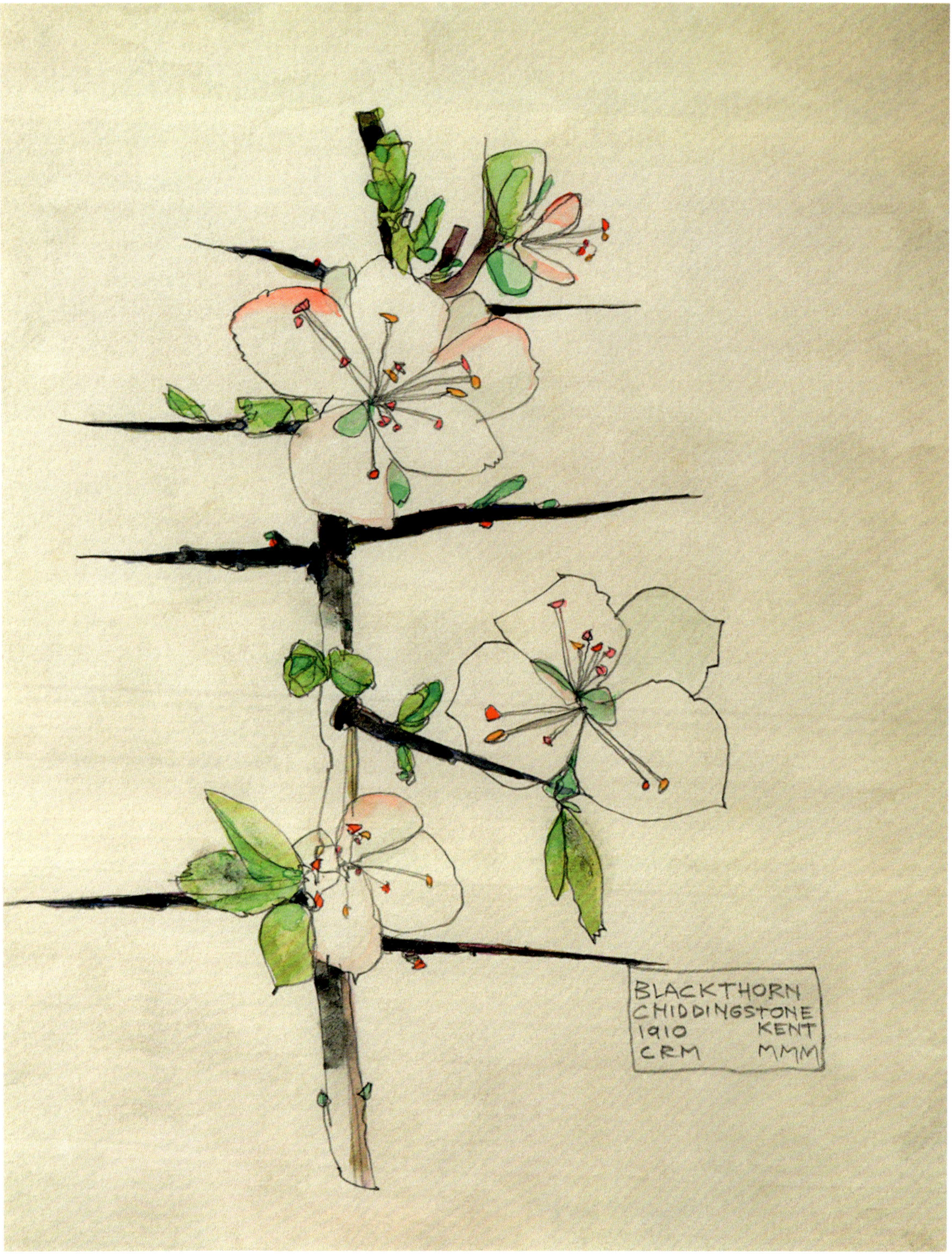
BLACKTHORN
CHIDDINGSTONE
1910 KENT
CRM MMM

CHARLES RENNIE MACKINTOSH (1868–1928)

Blackthorn

In the most exciting way Charles Rennie Mackintosh's flower studies sprang from the same skills that inspired his innovative architecture and design. From his beginnings as an evening student in the Glasgow School of Art in 1884, until he became the leading exponent of their style of Art Nouveau and architect of the new school and library, he drew flowers. In a lecture in 1902 he told his students to abandon all models and derivative ideas and use 'real flowers springing from your own soul'.

The soul that made this blackthorn (or any flower he painted) uniquely his, can be seen developing with his architectural drawings of the 1880s. Alongside field sketches of Scottish vernacular architecture which captured its characteristic grace and angularity, some nearby flower might be included using the same draughtsmanship and deftness of touch. In the 1890s Mackintosh began experimenting with highly stylised plant forms, especially his linear rose motifs which were adapted to many media from glass and metal to wood and printed fabrics. His botanical eye also inspired the interiors that he designed (including the four famous Glasgow Tea Rooms from 1897–1903), since the strict rectilinear lines of his furniture and accessories, and his monochrome environments, were enhanced by colours and curves based on plant structure. Japanese art was also an influence; Mackintosh owned oriental ceramics and prints, and discussions of Japanese graphic art emphasised that 'simplicity and reticence are apparent in all the best examples'.

In 1900 Mackintosh married his fellow student at Glasgow, Margaret Macdonald, and sketching holidays became an important feature of their lives. His flower watercolours have an inscription cartouche reading Holy Island, Scilly, Walberswick, or in this case Chiddingstone, where, early in 1910, they stayed in the Kentish Weald (where blackthorn still fills the springtime hedgerows). Mackintosh also sketched Kentish oast houses, again marrying architecture and plants, and leaving areas of his finished work untouched by watercolour. The effect was both practical and beautiful, because it revealed the patterns, textures and contrasts of overlapping forms.

Blackthorn, Chiddingstone, Kent 1910
Pencil and watercolour on paper,
25.8 x 20 cm
Private collection

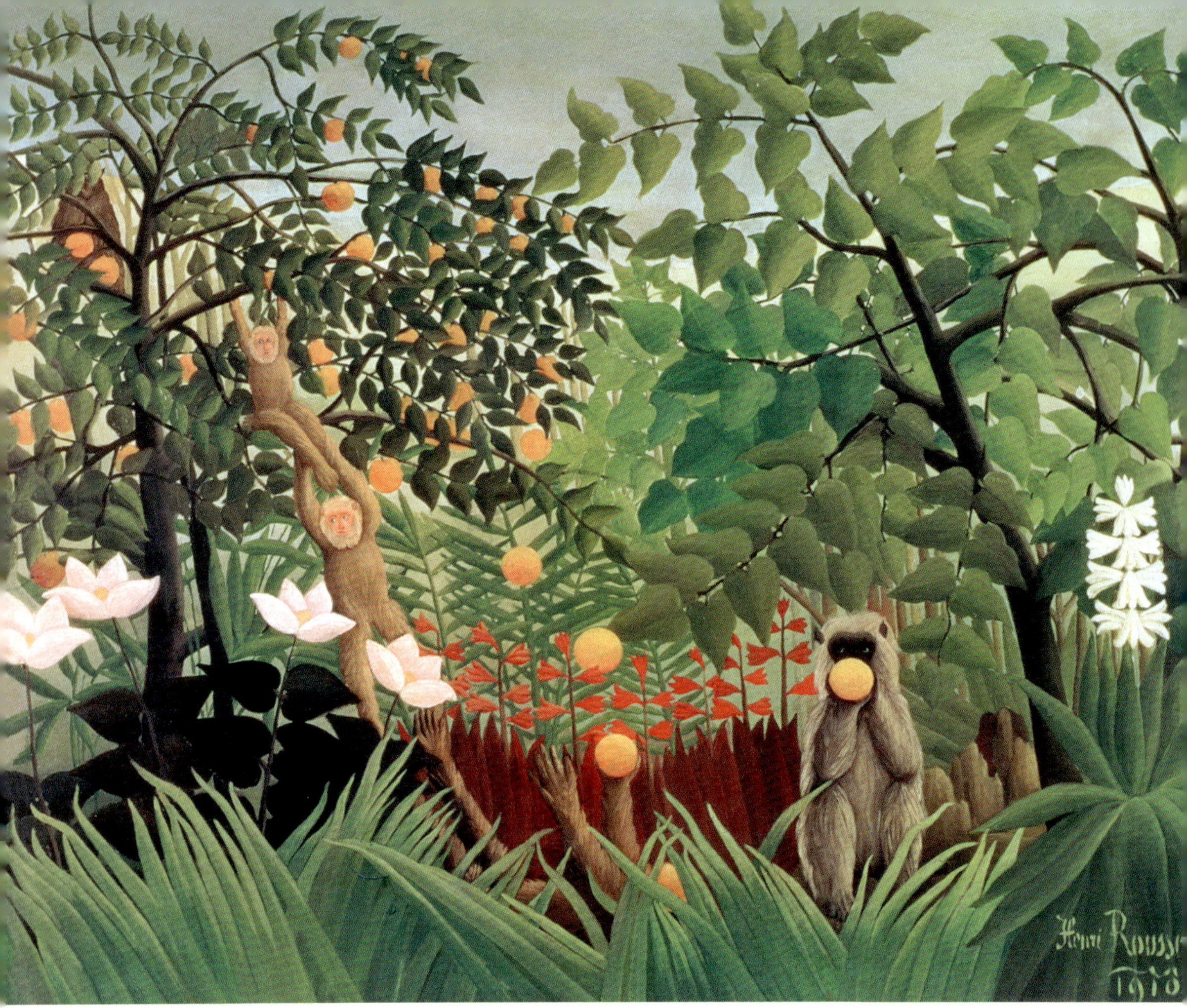

Exotic Landscape 1910
Oil on canvas, 130 x 162 cm
Norton Simon Collection, Pasadena

HENRI ROUSSEAU (1844–1910)

Lotus flowers

In 1908 Picasso held a mock banquet in Rousseau's honour; the poet Apollinaire declaimed, 'You remember Rousseau the land of the Aztecs, the forests where mangoes and pineapples grow', and the tipsy old artist replied to Picasso, 'We are the two great painters of the age, you in the Egyptian style and me in the modern'. Rousseau's naive jungles, and his dream-like mixture of the real and unreal, opened the way for Surrealist art. He first won a critic's praise in 1891: 'his tiger surprising its prey in a storm ought not to be missed; it is the alpha and omega of painting'. It did not matter that these predatory animals were copied from illustrations in adventure books – they evoked a similar fascination with far-away primitive lands – but without Rousseau's dense foliage they would have lacked their mystery, beauty and menace. In 1905 he exhibited alongside Matisse's group, and probably helped to earn them the name Fauves (meaning wild beasts) by association with the creatures which leapt, swung and devoured each other in Rousseau's forests.

The plants that Rousseau painted were recognisable, although he had never travelled anywhere more tropical than the hothouses of the botanic garden in Paris and he sometimes placed bunches of bananas upside-down on the wrong trees. As a playground for these surreal monkeys swinging from an orange tree and using the fruit as balls, he set the Asian lotus alongside the American yucca, in a jungle where neither would grow, with a foreground thicket of African sansevieria. But in combining these plants Rousseau's sense of colour and composition was unique and sublime. The lotus appealed to his artist's eye for the stately way the immense flowers rise above the surface of the water. (In 1907 he actually painted lotus growing in a lake, but this time with flamingos, another lovely but unnatural juxtaposition). Here, among his primeval trees, the lotus becomes a fantasy flower, creating globes of light, and turning nightmare into fairyland.

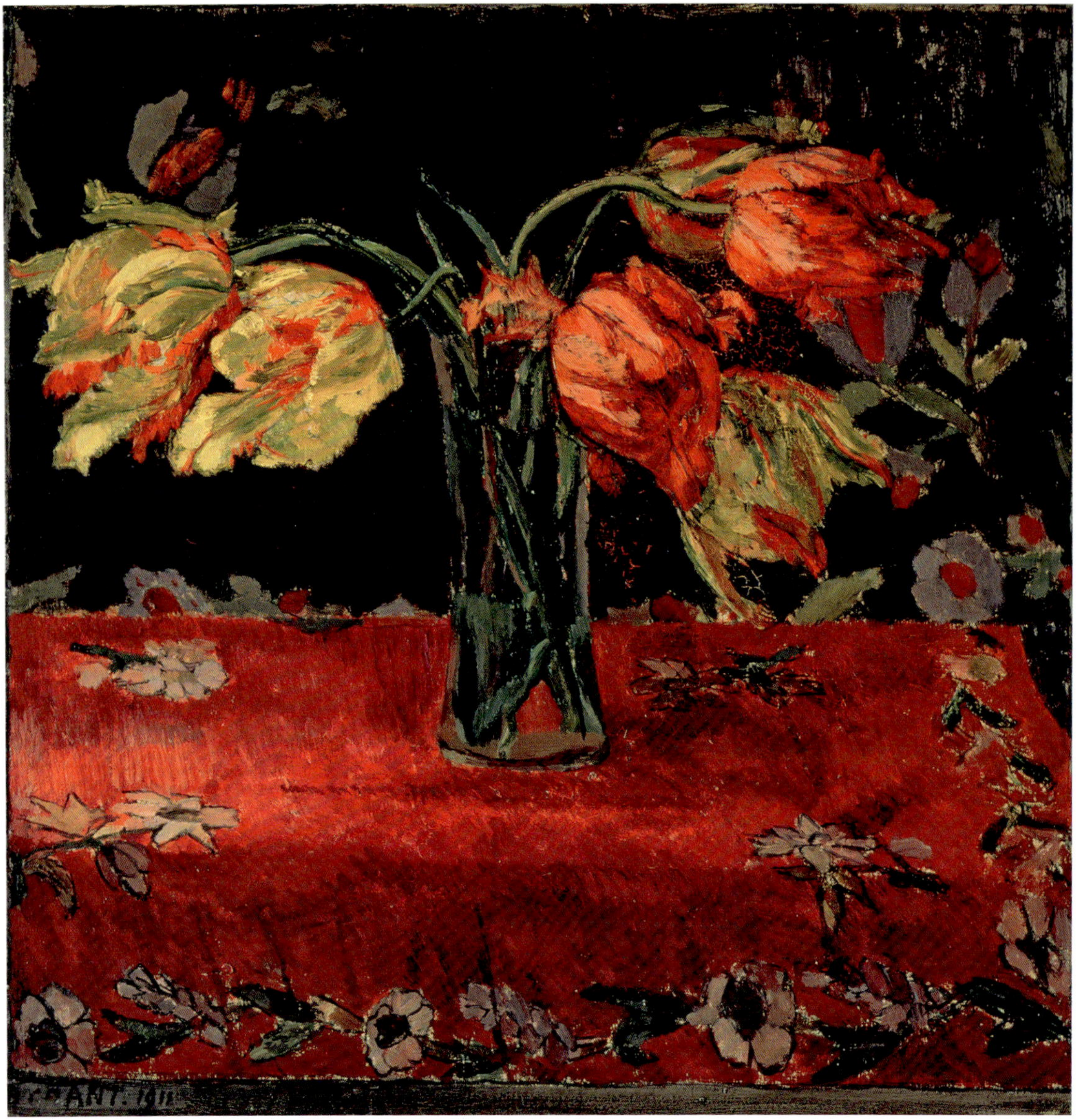

Parrot Tulips 1911
Oil on canvas, 52 x 49 cm
Southampton City Art Gallery

DUNCAN GRANT (1885–1978)

Tulips

When Duncan Grant painted this vase of shining red and yellow tulips there was nothing new about the flowers – for centuries they had been the darlings of flower painters – but he displayed them in a manner as vivid and unconventional as his own lifestyle. In 1911 the painting was exhibited alongside works by other members of Walter Sickert's Camden Town Group, who all admired Van Gogh and Gauguin, but none could emulate their use of colour as Grant did. In that same decade he established himself as an adventurous and experimental British artist. He was involved with Roger Fry's two post-Impressionist exhibitions (which introduced London to Cézanne, Picasso and Matisse) and was the leading designer in Fry's Omega Workshops (creating textiles, ceramics and furniture with bold, asymmetrical patterns).

In this painting the strongest influence was Matisse, who also loved to crowd his interiors with patterned fabrics, creating a joyous contrast between real flowers and the naive outlines of the unreal. Grant has used the latter as playful blobs of blue and pink to relieve the heavy red tablecloth and the dark background, producing an effect that makes the tulips swirl instead of droop. It is a fine example of how colours can grow stronger by dramatising the background, rather than neutralising it as the old masters did. And the bright green among the streaks of red and yellow on the tulip petals is an extra delight for those who recognise the mark of an ancestral strain known as 'viridiflora'.

By 1911 Grant was a member of the Bloomsbury Group, first introduced by his cousin and lover Lytton Strachey, and blessed with such wit, charm and sultry good looks that he could enjoy affairs simultaneously with whatever man or woman took his fancy. By 1913 Vanessa Bell too was irresistibly drawn to him, and began a lifelong partnership in which they lived and painted together with such mutual understanding that his infidelities faded into insignificance.

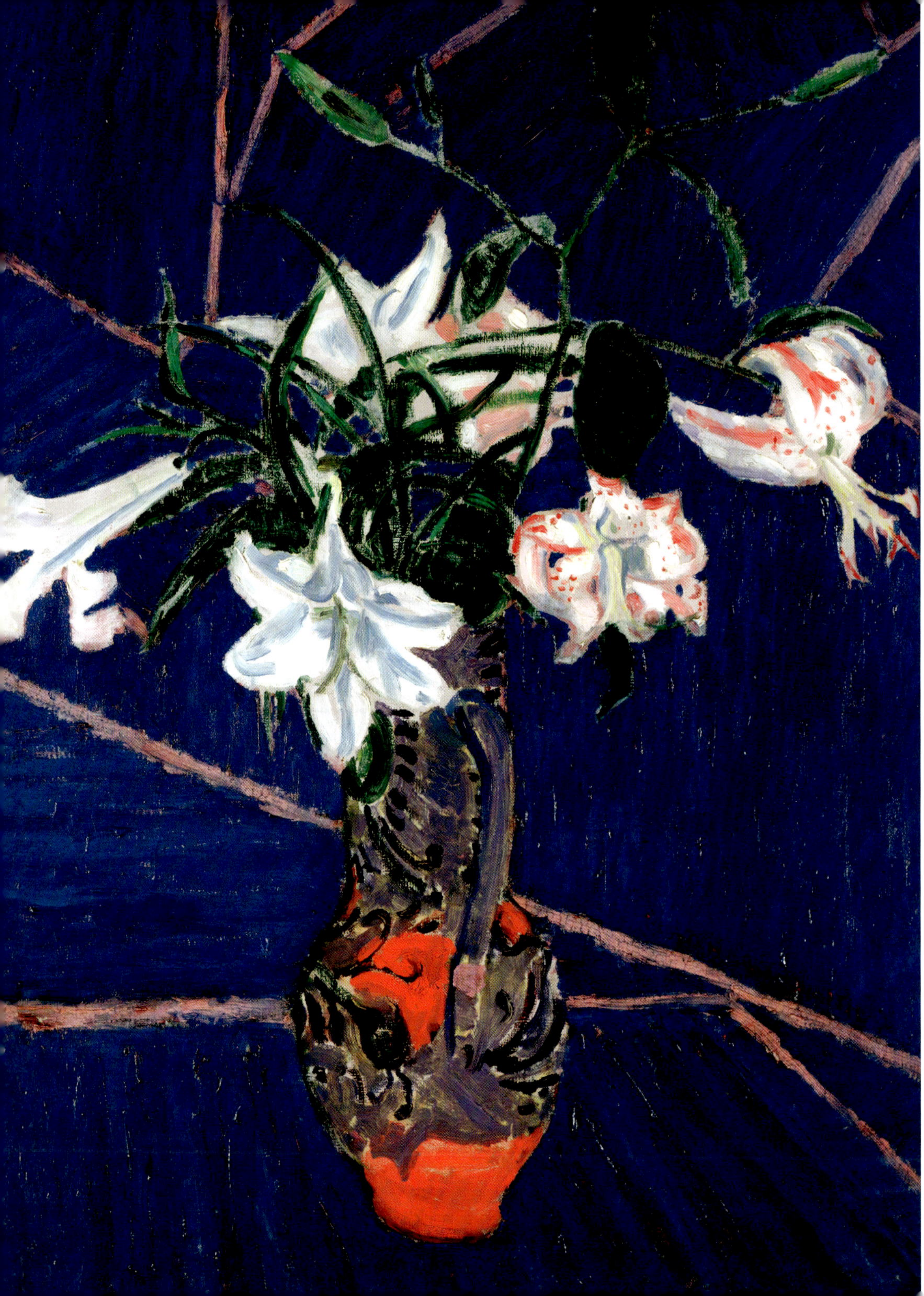

MATTHEW SMITH (1879–1959)

Lilies

Matthew Smith claimed his life began in 1908, when he escaped from his Yorkshire manufacturing family and joined the artists' colony in Brittany, where Gauguin himself had first learnt to substitute bright, saturated colours for dull reality. Matisse and Derain continued this avant-garde tradition, which had been included under various titles including Symbolist and neo-Impressionist, until in 1905 the term Fauves – meaning wild beasts – was coined by an art critic viewing their exhibition at the Paris Salon. After spending a year in Brittany, Matthew Smith proceeded to Paris (briefly studying under Matisse in 1911) and he too fell under the spell of their intense colours.

Later he wrote of his own critics, 'They all praise the colour, but there is something else I think', by which he meant the importance of structure. Behind the lilies, which were painted at the end of that first youthful experience in France, his underlying design with its thin lines of pink remains excitingly obvious. Originally the lines served to sketch in the table and the perspective of the walls, to centre the vase and its flowers. Then their bright pink colour helped to emphasise the stripes and spots on the lilies against the challenging blue of the background, while their diagonal geometry enhanced the spiky vitality of the leaves and petals of the lilies; and possibly Matthew Smith had encountered the dramatic perspective lines and shadows of the Surrealist artist de Chirico, his contemporary in Paris.

There are two kinds of lily in the vase; a type known as Turk's cap with recurved petals and of oriental origin – the splashes of pink on their white petals suggest either *Lilium auratum* or *Lilium speciosum*, both from Japan. The other, a trumpet-shaped lily, is as pure white as the traditional Madonna lily, *Lilium candidum*, although it too may be one of the newer nineteenth-century introductions of Asiatic lilies, possibly *Lilium longiflorum* also from Japan.

Lilies 1913–14
Oil on canvas, 73.6 x 53.2 cm
City Art Gallery, Leeds
Museums and Galleries

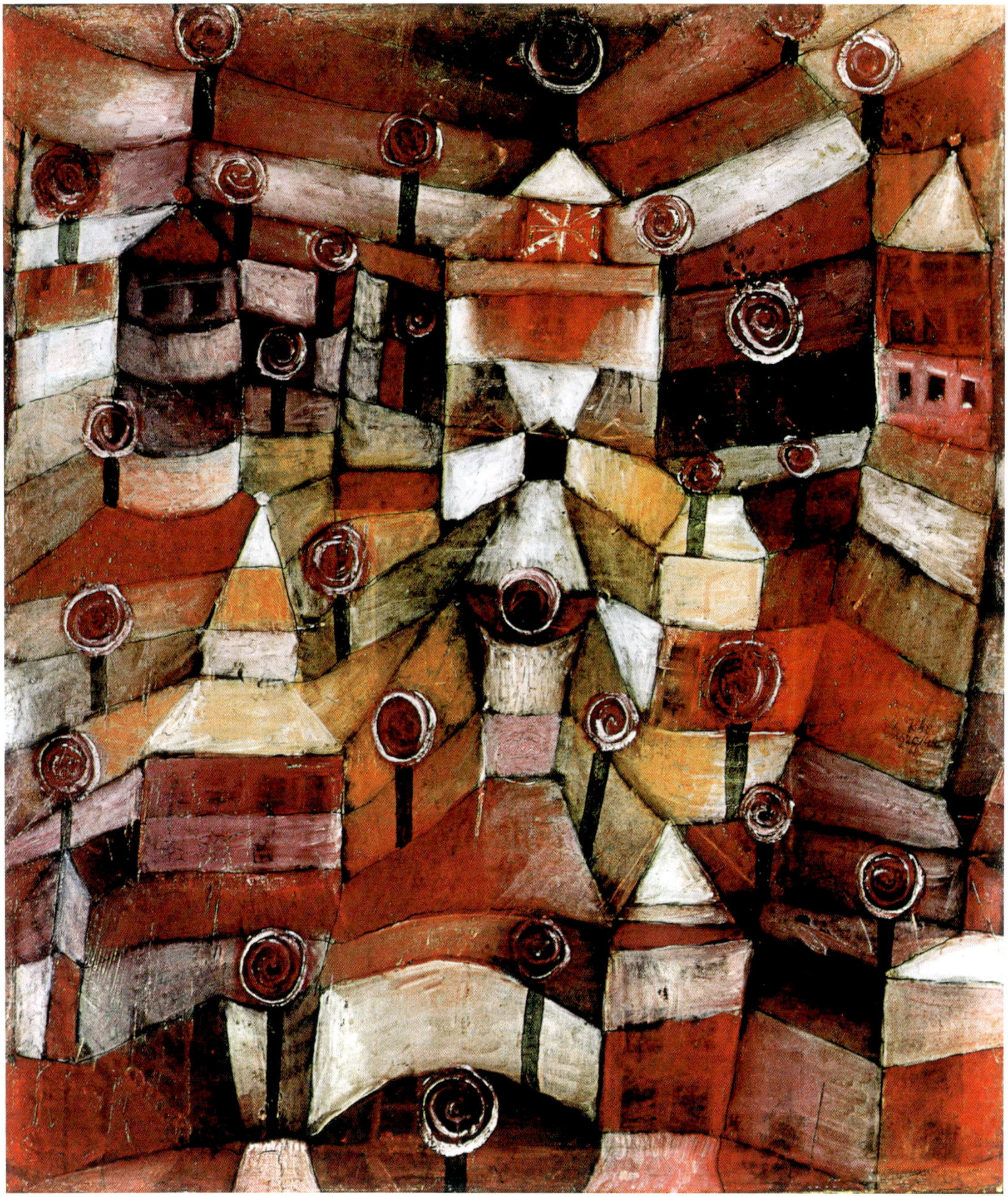

The Rose Garden 1920
Oil on cardboard, 49 x 42.5 cm
Städtische Galerie, Munich

PAUL KLEE (1879–1940)

Roses

The originality of Paul Klee's rose garden is captivating because of its contradictions. His exploration of early twentieth-century artistic styles, including Abstraction and Cubism, dispels any of the sweet banalities that might cling to such gardens. And yet the painting is extremely evocative of walking along formal pathways among rose bushes.

All the shades of red and pink, the cream, white and yellow of rose petals are here. Besides, there is a strong element of myth and fairy tale as the eye is led past the spiralling bushes and the mysterious buildings. Where is it leading? This is the world of lost heroines, of Beauty and the Beast or Sleeping Beauty, and the fear of enchantment, as well as its lure, is intense.

How could this sensation be achieved with such unreal forms? Part of the secret, according to Klee, lay in following the rhythms and mathematical constructions that were inherent in nature, music and art. Klee almost became a musician, and when he turned to painting he shared these concepts with Robert Delaunay, whom he visited in Paris in 1912, and Wassily Kandinsky, whom he joined in the second Blue Rider exhibition in Munich that same year. According to the artists espousing this theory, the use of colour as well as line was essential for capturing these innate harmonies; and for Klee a visit to Tunisia in 1914, absorbing the brilliance of the light, was his apotheosis. 'Now colour possesses me,' he wrote, 'I no longer need to pursue it, colour and I are one – I am a painter.'

By the time Klee painted *The Rose Garden* he was internationally famous. In 1921 he started teaching at the Bauhaus and publishing his theories, until the Nazis forced his return to Switzerland in 1933. 'Taking a line for a walk' is his best remembered precept, and in his paintings he filled each step with new and colourful meaning.

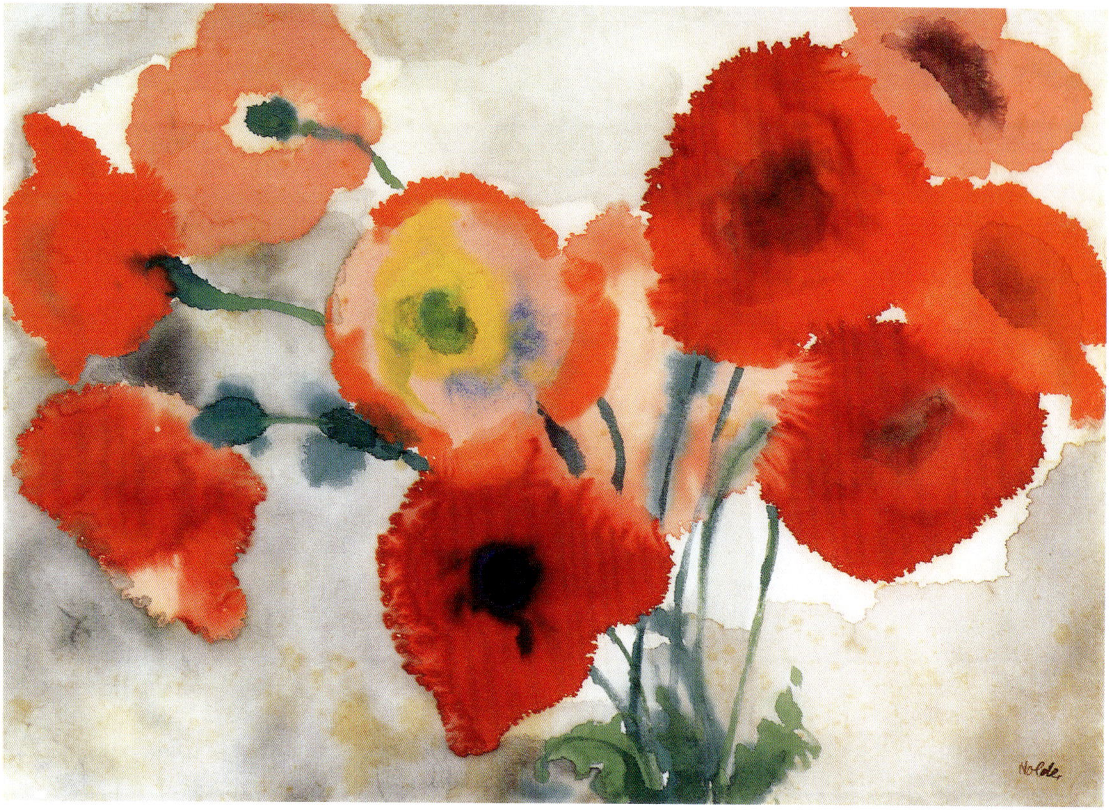

Red Poppies 1920
Watercolour on Japanese tissue,
34.3 x 47.9 cm
Philadelphia Museum of Art

EMIL NOLDE (1867–1956)

Poppies

Poppies seem magical flowers, not only for the intense red light shining through their petals, but because they are narcotic. Syrup of poppies was processed for pain relief from these red petals (although the latex of oriental opium poppies is more powerful and more lethal). Being supernatural, poppies were associated with ancient goddesses of death and fertility, and their characteristic of springing up in battlefields, turning gruesome memories into a shining sea of red, has kept their folklore fresh through generations.

No twentieth-century artist was better suited to express this hidden potential than Emil Nolde. Born in the German-Danish borderlands (he took his name from the village of Nolde) to devout Protestant parents, he had much in common with Van Gogh, the predecessor he most admired for pouring his difficult emotions into vibrant paintings. Nolde never belonged with a group, but he was inspired by his contemporaries in the German Expressionist movement, and from 1906 he exhibited alongside them. His most powerful work explored the supernatural – including biblical imagery and arresting landscapes – using grotesque distortions and violent colours which could be regarded as ecstatic or brutalised.

All his life Nolde loved flowers and created gardens. In painting them his savagery was mitigated into intense but sensitive appreciation. In answer to the criticism that he exaggerated their colour he said, 'I once positioned my canvases among the flowers themselves and saw immediately how much they paled compared to nature'. His first important flower painting, *Violette Blumen* of 1907, was inspired by the fishermens' gardens in the Baltic island of Alsen, where he and his wife Ada eventually planted a garden of their own.

Nolde was a master of both oils and watercolours describing 'the continuous chain of little inventions and technical discoveries of one's own'. One of these took place when he discovered Japanese paper (the most wonderfully absorbent medium) in Berlin in 1916, and perfected the method of working watercolours 'wet on wet', which is the secret behind his magical poppies.

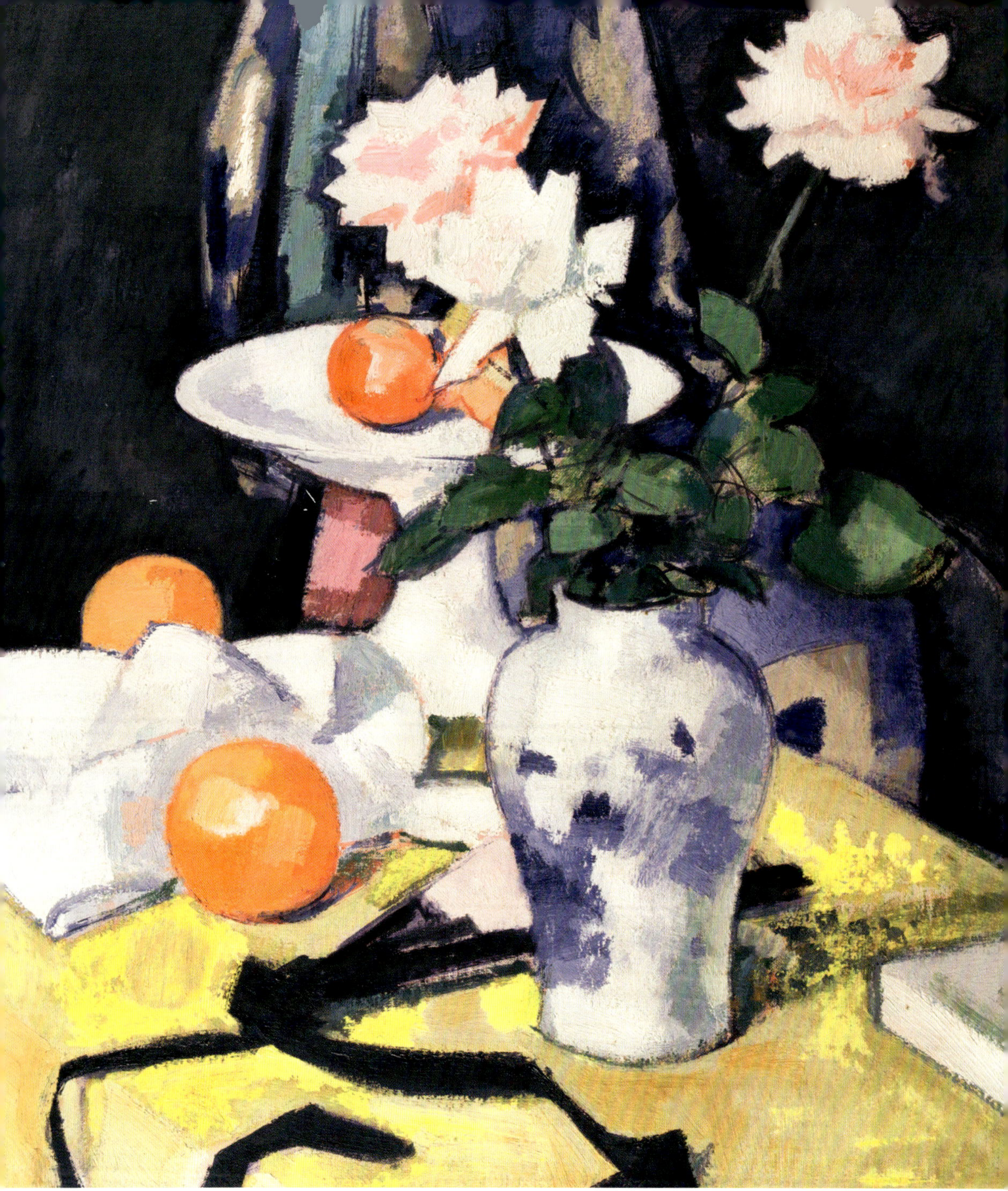

SAMUEL PEPLOE (1871–1935)

Roses

Samuel Peploe was intent on producing the perfect still life and would spend weeks setting up various objects in his Edinburgh studio, calmly reassessing their positions, analysing them for colour harmony and balance, until all was exactly as he wished. Since roses would not have submitted to this prolonged treatment, their living freshness must have been captured by some other method, and it is this spontaneous ingredient which adds magic to the painting.

Peploe belonged to the Scottish Colourists, a group of four artists who continued the work of the Glasgow Boys, grafting their own knowledge of contemporary French art onto their more staid traditions of painting. Peploe's first visits to France and Holland, and his first solo exhibition in Edinburgh, took place in the early 1900s, but from 1910–12 he joined another Colourist, J.D. Fergusson, and remained longer in Paris. Among the discernible influences on Peploe's work are Manet's dramatic use of black and the lovely, liquid paint effects on the rose petals; Cézanne's device of a folded background textile merging into a darker blue wall; and Matisse's daring way of crowding colour and pattern. There is even a touch of Cubism in the angles Peploe has created, although his earlier and more obvious experiments have been successfully submerged in the overall effect. As for the orient, the blue and white vase was part of Peploe's collection which he often featured, and his sense of line, colour and pattern had been liberated (directly or indirectly) by the Japanese prints that flooded the Paris art market.

Peploe was at the height of his powers in the 1920s, the period to which this painting belongs. The final element distinguishing his mature style was his confident use of clear, reflecting white. Although he spent most of the year working in his Edinburgh studio, his summers were spent in the Scottish islands and the south of France, often with Francis Cadell, another Colourist, absorbing the freshness and shimmering light that were reflected in his still lifes.

Roses and Oranges c.1920
Oil on canvas, 55.9 x 50.9 cm
Private collection

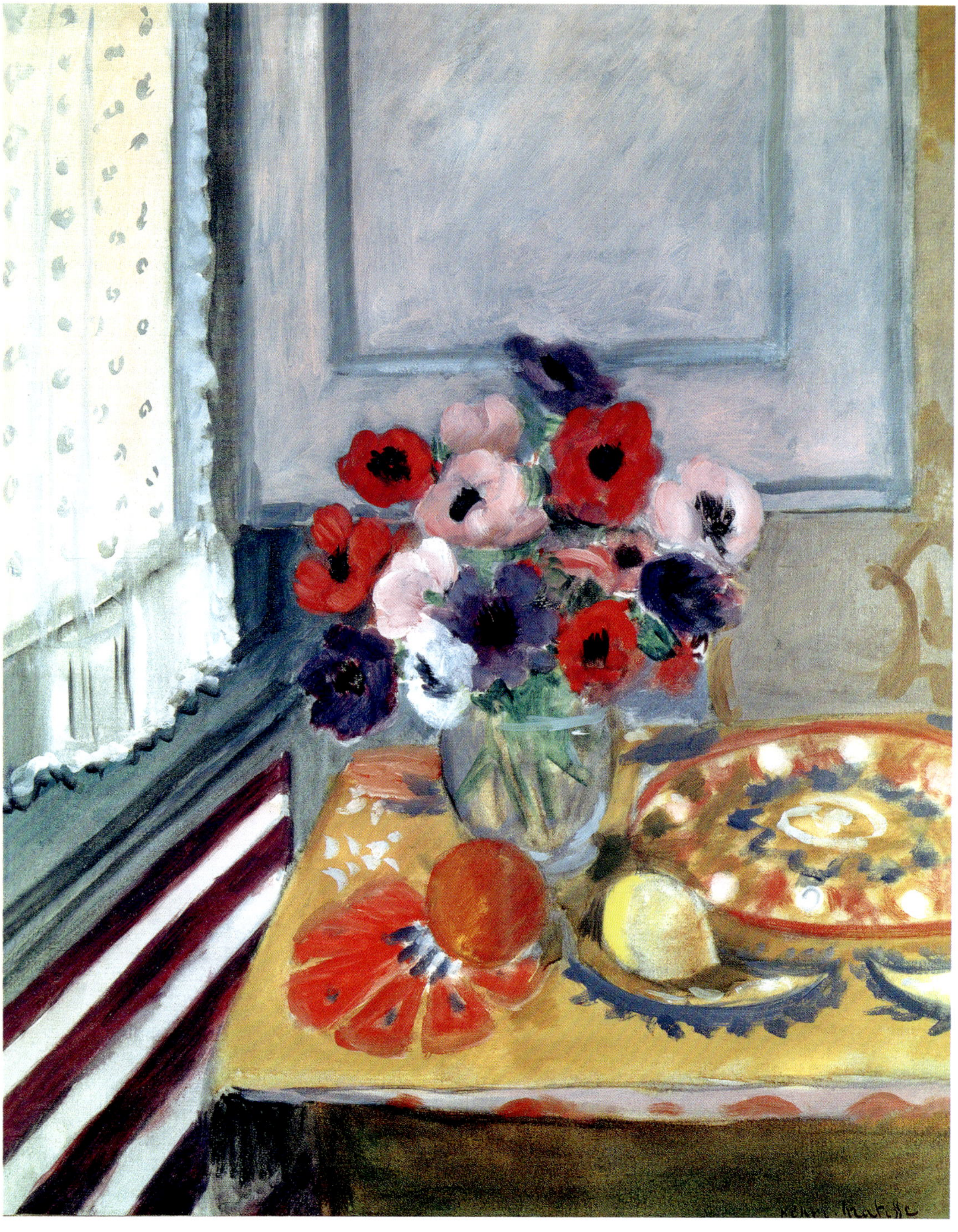

HENRI MATISSE (1869–1954)

Anemones

Flowers for Matisse were the focal point of composite patterns. Around his anemones the swirling lines and blocks of colour have been assembled with such fluency – their pink and purple petals echoed on the background, their blues and reds in the textiles, while their pure blacks and whites command the centre. Matisse may have loved anemones especially for this smudge of black, for he painted them often, and always captured the particular way they sit in a vase, either revealing their black hearts or hiding them.

Matisse first succumbed to bright colour while painting in Brittany in 1896; he bought the work of other great colourists such as Cézanne, Gauguin, Van Gogh and Redon, and by 1905 he was the leader of the Fauves who – in an age accustomed to Impressionism – still caused a sensation with their vivid and exaggerated use of colour. From 1906 when he first visited Algeria (and painted *Joie de Vivre*) Matisse was also enchanted by orientalism. He made repeated visits to North Africa and started to create the 'elaborate fictions' of his Odalisques – harem women, nude or clothed in silks – surrounded by the screens, carpets and costumes of the East. For patterns Matisse used the fabrics he amassed on his travels, such as the Moroccan tablecloth here spread under the anemones, and flowers fitted as luxuriantly into these exotic surroundings as did his female models.

All his life Matisse was an avid collector of fabrics, and after 1917, when he lived mainly in Nice, his various studios overflowed with patterns which he called 'my working library'. This love of design went right back to his childhood, growing up in the textile manufacturing towns near the Belgian border, where for generations his ancestors had been weavers.

Moving to the South of France, where he painted the anemones, brought a final luminous serenity to Matisse's work, his patterning remained strong but not agitated. 'I have always wished', he said, 'that my work would have the lightness and gaiety of spring without giving a hint of the effort it has cost.'

Anemones 1924
Oil on canvas, 71 x 56.5 cm
Private collection

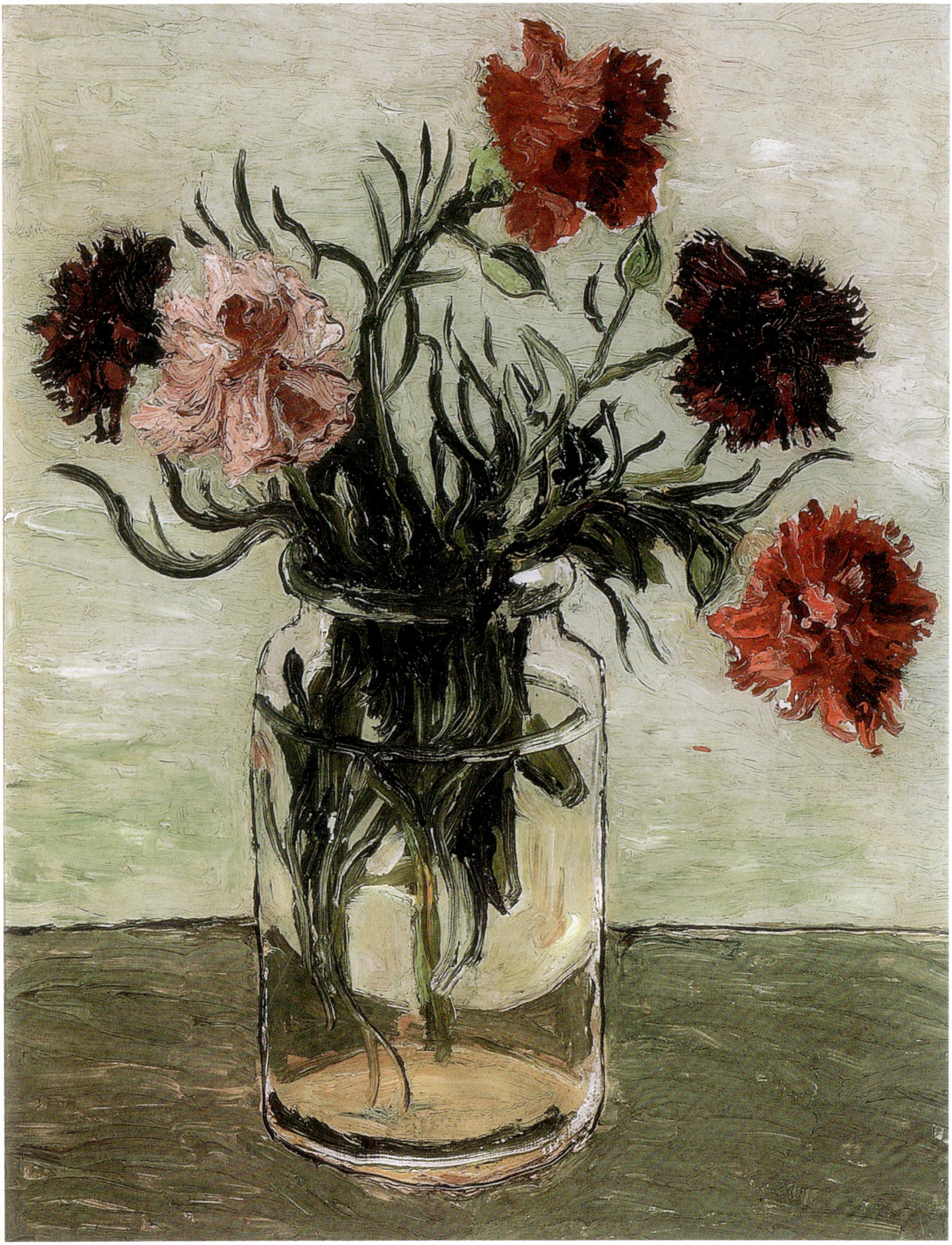

CHRISTOPHER WOOD (1901–1930)

Carnations

Pinks and carnations are among the great traditional flowers of Western art. Leonardo and Raphael included them in paintings of the Virgin and Child; they decorated the backgrounds of millefleurs tapestries, the borders of illuminated manuscripts and the embroidered dresses of ladies in court portraits. From small pink flowers they can be traced developing into red and white, until in seventeenth-century flower paintings they burst forth in a mass of petals and striking mixtures of all three colours. The finest blooms were horticultural treasures, listed in catalogues with grandiose names, while the simpler pinks were used as flavourings (like cloves) and sometimes appear in still lifes scattered on salads or stuck into pastries.

But they did not appear like this, alone in a vase, until Christopher Wood devoted one of his finest paintings to them; nor had they ever seemed more darkly purple or more richly red, nor the buds such a fresh, bursting green. The secret rests in the luminous background, formed of hasty brushstrokes, irregularly reflected in the glass and water of the vase, infusing the painting with energy and light.

All Wood's work was experimental and, since he was an opium addict, based on heightened sensation. His tragically short life was an exciting one. He travelled to Paris to paint in 1921, and there fell under the spell of Antonio de Gandarillas, a glamorous Chilean diplomat who became his lover and introduced him into fashionable artistic circles, including Diaghilev of the *Ballets Russes* for whom Picasso was also working. Between 1925 and 1926 Wood exhibited his work in Paris and London, and met Ben and Winifred Nicholson (Wood's flower paintings have much in common with hers). With them in Cornwall he discovered the naive charms of Alfred Wallis's coastal paintings. But after 1927 he entered a downward spiral of mental and financial instability ending in suicide – becoming a legendary genius cut off before his prime. A life celebrated in Sebastian Faulks's *The Fatal Englishman*.

Carnations in a Glass Jar 1925
Oil on board, 33 x 26.6 cm
Private collection

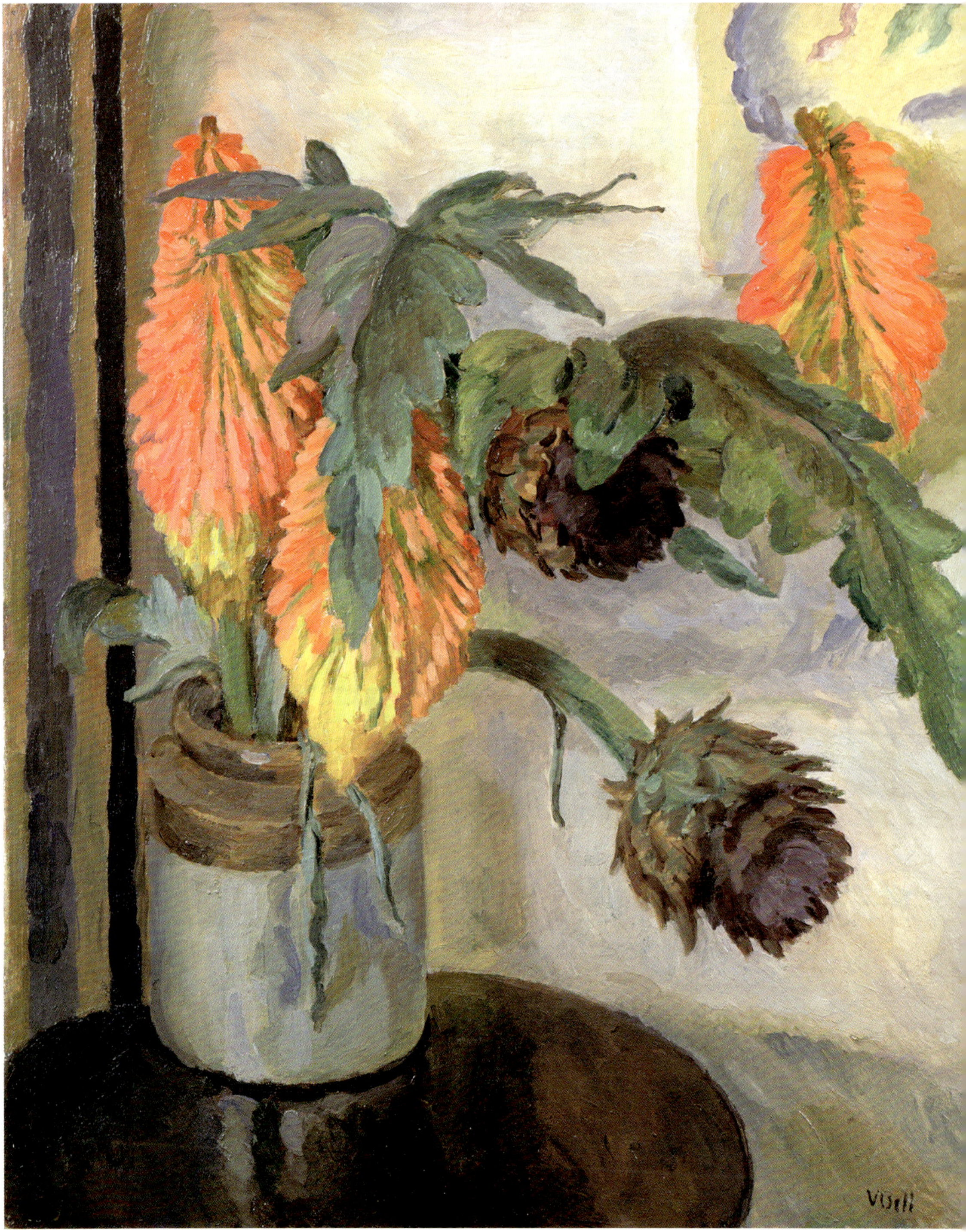
VBell

VANESSA BELL (1879–1961)

Red hot pokers and artichokes

Vanessa Bell's skill in using asymmetrical patterns and earth colours is evident in this painting. The setting perfectly complements the flowers – the dark curve of the table and the vertical stripes in the wall hold the flowing lines of leaf and stem, the glowing pokers and the sombre artichokes, like the rhythms of the contemporary dances that Vanessa loved. The painting echoes the sophistication of the Bloomsbury set, and Vanessa's work as a textile designer for Roger Fry's Omega workshop, but even more it represents her life at Charleston and all its bold, unconventional creativity. She discovered the Sussex farmhouse in 1916, nestling beneath the South Downs near the country home of her sister Virginia Woolf, and moved in with her two young sons and fellow spirit Duncan Grant, escaping from wartime London and her husband Clive Bell.

The decade had begun with Roger Fry's groundbreaking exhibitions of Post-Impressionist art which introduced London to Picasso and Matisse. For Vanessa they were a revelation, opening up a world of abstract forms, challenging patterns and dramatic colours – but above all she admired Cézanne, nicknaming him 'The holy man of Aix'. His influence shows strongly in the forward tilt of the table; the muted, roughly-blended colours of the wall; and the choice of a plain earthenware jar (which was also entirely practical for holding such heavy flowers).

Roger Fry was a frequent visitor to Charleston and he helped reorder the garden within a framework of gravel paths and box hedges. Then Vanessa and Duncan planted the flowers with vibrant colours and messy growth habits which they both loved, calmed by the silver-blues of lavender and artichokes. There is a photo dated 1927 showing Duncan Grant with his daughter Angelica both dwarfed by the red hot pokers, and in August 1930 Vanessa wrote jubilantly to Roger Fry, 'the garden is full of reds...pokers are coming out and masses of plums and apples'; and a week later, 'I'm painting flowers, one can't resist them'. Perhaps this was the very painting.

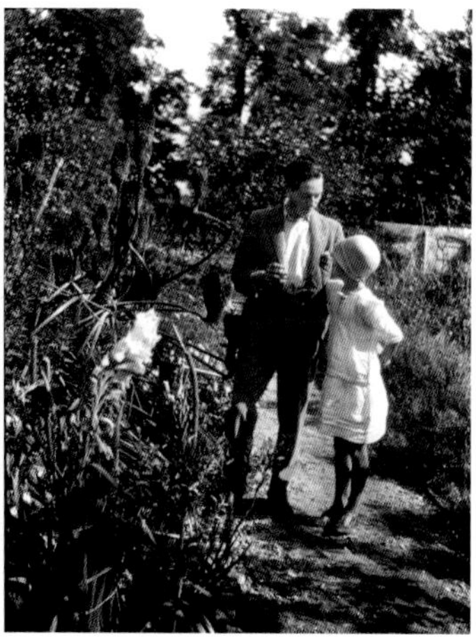

Duncan Grant and Angelica Bell in the garden at Charleston 1927
Photographic print

Red Hot Pokers c.1930
Oil on canvas, 66 x 53.3 cm
Private collection

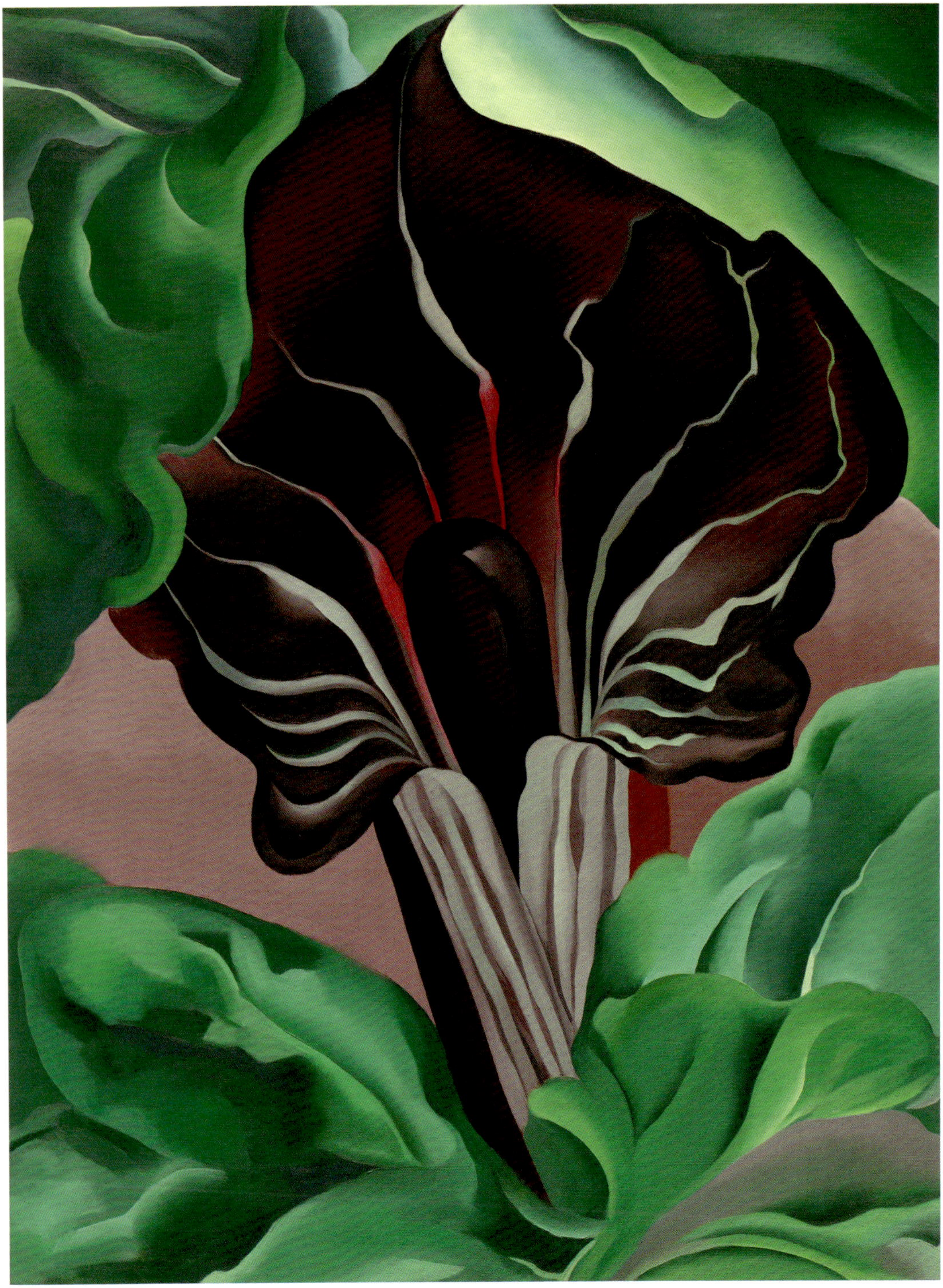

GEORGIA O'KEEFFE (1887–1986)

Jack-in-the-pulpit

No nickname given to arums, with their sexy purple spadix, was innocent. 'Lords-and-ladies' signified copulation, 'cuckoo-pint' was short for pintle, meaning penis. Cuckoo was a simplification of the Latin *cucullus*, a hooded cloak such as monks wore, referring to the large spathe enclosing the flower. It was this that led to a mocking link with priests – the English nickname was 'priest-in-a-pulpit', and the common American name became 'Jack-in-a-pulpit'.

The same aura of sexuality pervades Georgia O'Keeffe's stunning paintings of flowers, where the entire canvas is devoted to one bloom in extreme close-up, with the outer edges of the petals or leaves generally cut off. Such concentration needed technical perfection, O'Keeffe created dense invisible brushstrokes on very fine canvas, enabling her to capture the waxy white texture of calla lilies, the velvety nuances of colour at the heart of an iris, the swirl of rose petals, or the flame of red poppies. Zooming with great intensity towards the part of a flower where its reproductive organs lay evoked natural, but nevertheless startling, affinities with human anatomy. O'Keeffe's series of iris paintings became even more reminiscent of female genitalia than the arums and calla lilies were of the male.

Photography was an important influence, with the same power of creating dramatic close-ups. In 1916, soon after she arrived in New York (her family home was in Wisconsin) O'Keeffe met Alfred Stieglitz, the gallery owner and photographic artist, who used O'Keeffe – in dramatic close-up and often nude – as his model. In 1924, soon after their marriage, she started painting gigantic flowers. In this same period the skyscrapers of New York were under construction and she also painted these, often brilliantly lit at night. It was part of the same compulsion to come very close to the subject (whether it was small or large) and make it monumental, which inspired her painting for the rest of her life, whether of desert landscapes or dried animal bones. 'By emphasis', she said, 'we get at the real meaning of things.'

Jack-in-the-Pulpit No. II 1930
Oil on canvas, 101.6 x 76.2 cm
National Gallery of Art, Washington

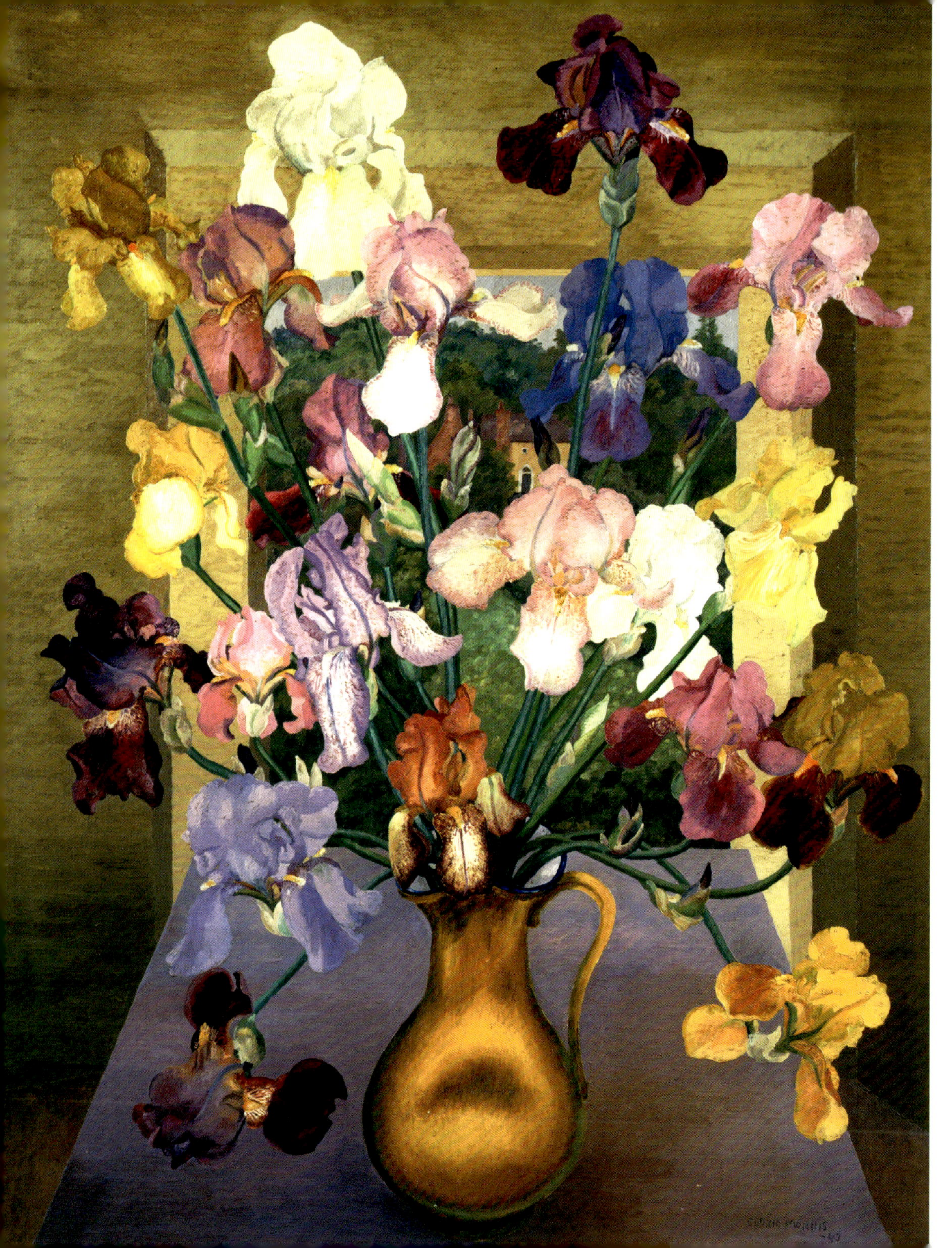

CEDRIC MORRIS (1889–1982)

Irises

Cedric Morris and his partner Lett Haines created the East Anglian School of Painting, first at Dedham in the heart of Constable country, and then nearby at Benton End, with the view across a Suffolk valley just visible here behind the irises on the window ledge. Among the alumni of the art college who were to become famous (Lucien Freud, Maggi Hambling and Ivon Hitchens), the locals sent their teenagers to paint, or help weed Cedric's garden, or join Lett who presided over the kitchen. Here, in conditions of squalor and inebriation, he produced memorable meals for a large and shifting population of students and visitors. Vita Sackville-West came on a pilgrimage, Beth Chatto received her initial inspiration and Elizabeth David exchanged recipes. All received generous donations of plants including the famous irises.

Cedric Morris's deep love and understanding of flowers vibrated through his paintings. They generally rambled across the canvas as they did in the flower beds, an abundant mixture of red hot pokers, poppies, purple clematis and blue delphiniums, interspersed with slender rarities collected on his Mediterranean travels. But irises were his favourites and they made his reputation. Every year he hand-pollinated a selection from his collection and reared about a thousand seedlings in the walled kitchen garden (except in the war years when they had to make way for vegetables). The greatest challenge was to breed irises in shades of pink and apricot, which became a focus of attention at successive Chelsea Flower Shows. His first was named 'Edward Windsor', a partisan declaration just after the abdication, but most of his irises had the suffix 'Benton', after their garden of origin. The features that won accolades were their great variety of subtle colours and contrasting markings, combined with elegance of shape. However, this most famous iris painting, where the glow of the flowers is matched by their golden vase, is named *Iris Seedlings*, which suggests they were just a casual picking from that year's experimental crop.

Iris Seedlings 1943
Oil on canvas, 121.9 x 91.8 cm
Tate Gallery, London

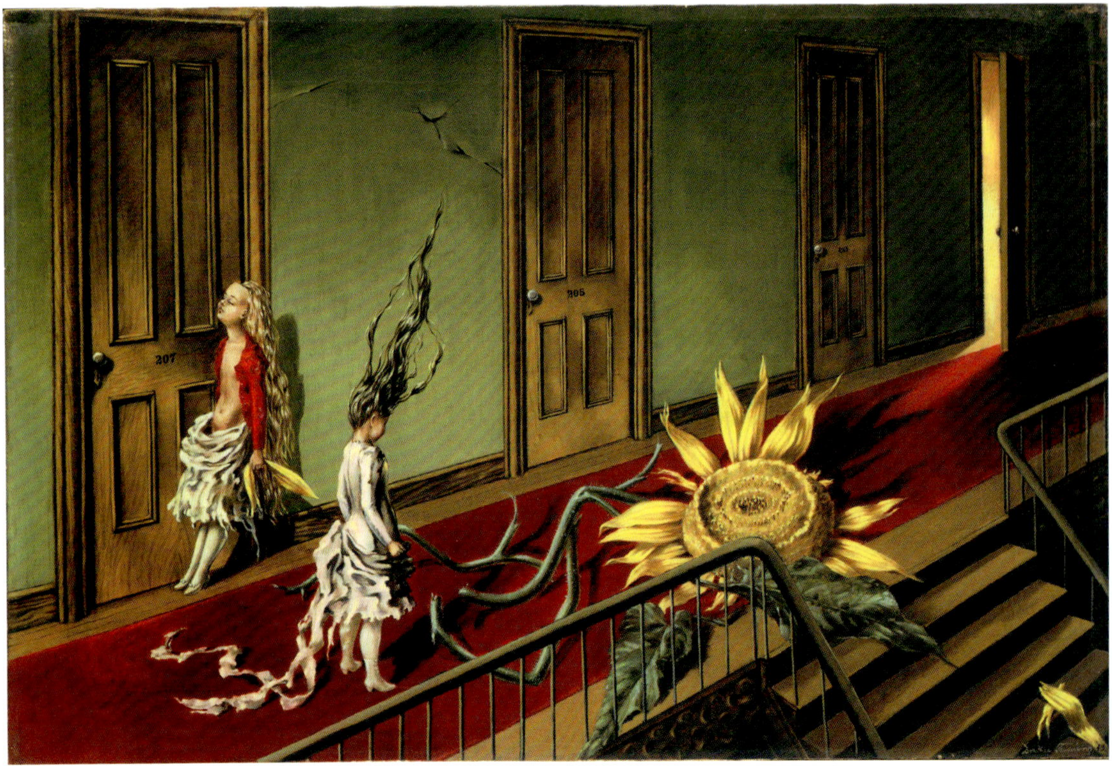

Eine Kleine Nachtmusik 1943
Oil on canvas, 40.7 x 61 cm
Tate Gallery, London

DOROTHEA TANNING (1910–2012)

Sunflower

Incongruous settings for familiar things – such as flowers – lie at the heart of Surrealist painting. Spread across the carpet of a hotel corridor, and confronting a young girl with torn clothes and her hair on end, the sunflower becomes monstrous. And yet it is a broken thing, its stems and leaves dismembered, shredded petals lying on the stairs, and another petal clutched in the hand of the lifelike doll leaning in the doorway like a fainting girl. In this nightmare of childhood fantasy, of dressing up and dreams of maturity, has the sunflower something to do with the line of yellow light emanating from the opening door? The scene seems all the more sinister because the artist named it *Eine Kleine Nachtmusik*, linking it with Mozart's light-hearted chamber music. Like the sunflower, it should be joyous.

Dorothea Tanning painted this, her masterpiece, when she was at the heart of the Surrealist movement in America. In 1935 she arrived in New York from Chicago, where she started her career designing theatre sets. The following year she was overwhelmed by the *Fantastic Art, Dada, Surrealism* exhibition at the Museum of Modern Art – describing the paintings as 'signposts so imperious, so laden, so seductive and yes, so perverse, that they would possess me utterly'. In 1941 the gallery owner Julien Levy started exhibiting her work, and he introduced her to eminent artists including Marcel Duchamp. In 1942 her self portrait *Birthday* explored similar themes to *Nachtmusik*, portraying her bare breasted in an elaborate blue jacket and skirt of twigs, standing before a long recession of open doors with a black, winged monster at her feet. The same year Max Ernst, the leading German Surrealist, visited her studio, stayed to play chess, and remained for the rest of his life. In 1946 they celebrated a double wedding with Man Ray (for whom Tanning modelled) and Juliet Browner. The couple moved to Arizona, and later to France, but when Max Ernst died in 1976, Tanning returned to New York and reached her one hundredth birthday in 2010.

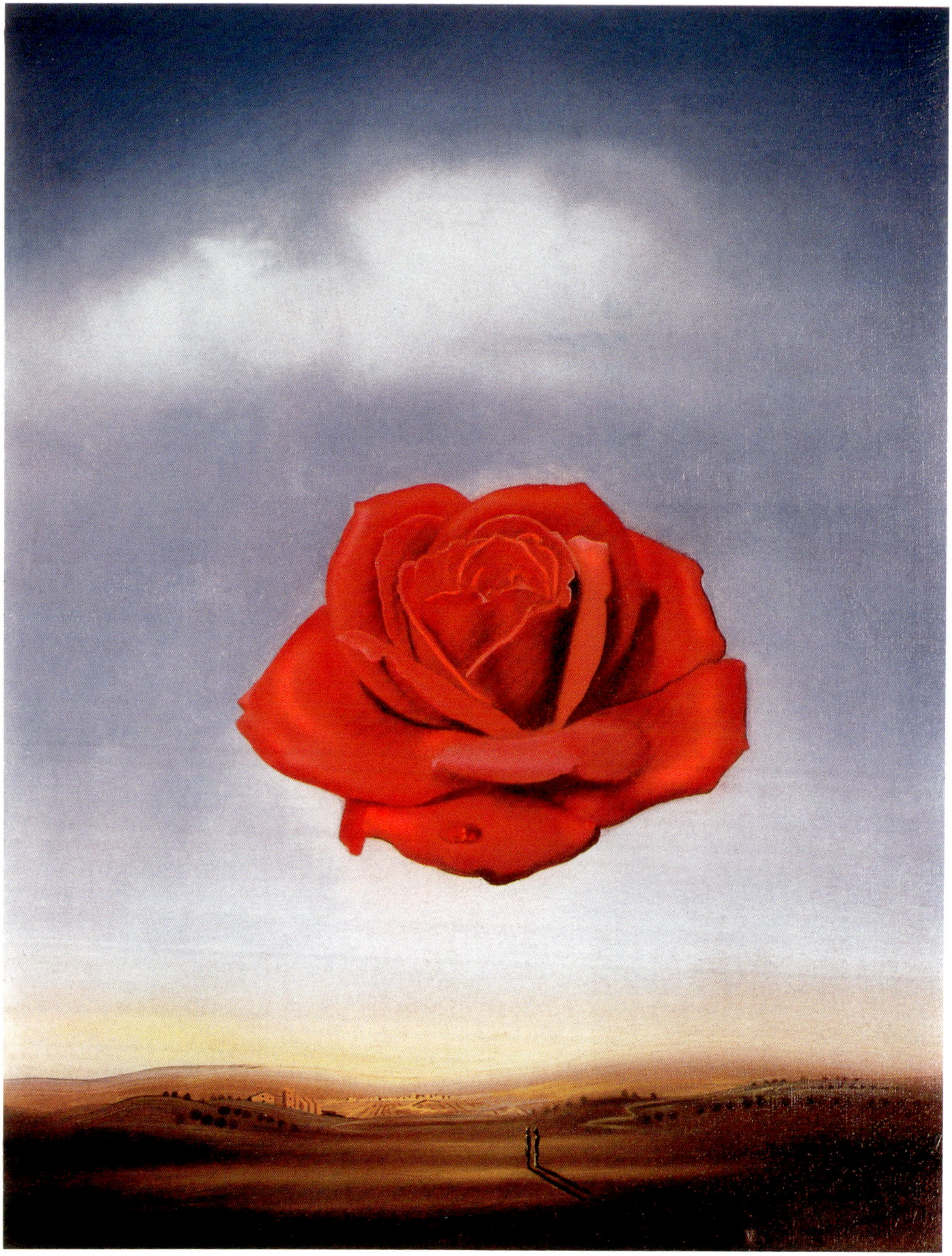

Meditative Rose 1958
Oil on canvas, 36 x 28 cm
Private collection

SALVADOR DALI (1904–1989)

Rose

In 1948 Dali returned from America, and the public parade of his eccentricities, to live for the rest of his life at Port Lligat, near his childhood home in Catalonia. His paintings still relied on what he termed 'paranoiac critical activity', using his subconscious to create groups of images which 'may or may not be susceptible to significant interpretation'. But in the 1950s Dali turned increasingly to traditional Christian imagery and mysticism, most notably with *Christ of St John of the Cross*, the magnificent vision of the Crucifixion against a black sky, slanting over a landscape with fishermen. The red rose he painted a few years later could be open to the same mystic interpretation, it floats in the sky like a heavenly manifestation, the blood red of its petals could signify martyrdom and crucifixion, the dewdrop could symbolise a tear of devotional grief. The Spanish landscape spread beneath the mystic rose is lit by evening light, and Dali's tiny praying couple are from Millet's iconic *Angelus* – a couple working in a field pausing to pray at sunset.

The pair were a recurring image in Dali's paintings. Usually they formed the background to an enigmatic or threatening encounter, once he turned them into melting white rocks, once the man became a skeleton, sometimes the woman seemed aggressive. Dali explained that as a schoolboy he discovered in the *Angelus* a wealth of emotions, but as an adult it disturbed him terribly. He claimed it represented 'a monstrous example of disguised sexual repression'. If this possibility is coupled with his earlier use of the red rose to replace women's heads, or wombs, or even flowing from them as menstrual blood, then the transcendental rose is compromised. Even the dewdrop is subject to Dali's surreal self-analysis – because he referred to his childhood trauma of having a dead brother, 'we resembled each other like two drops of water, but we had different reflections'. Dali's pain, ambiguity and revulsion are the heart of the matter – and of his rose.

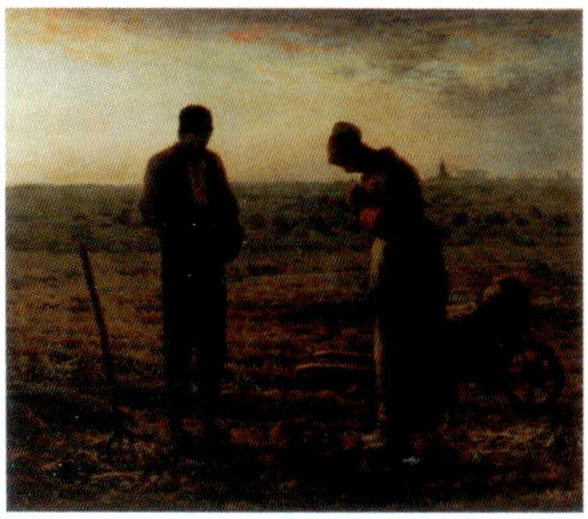

JEAN-FRANCOIS MILLET
Angelus 1857–59
Oil on canvas, 55.5 x 66 cm
Musée d'Orsay, Paris

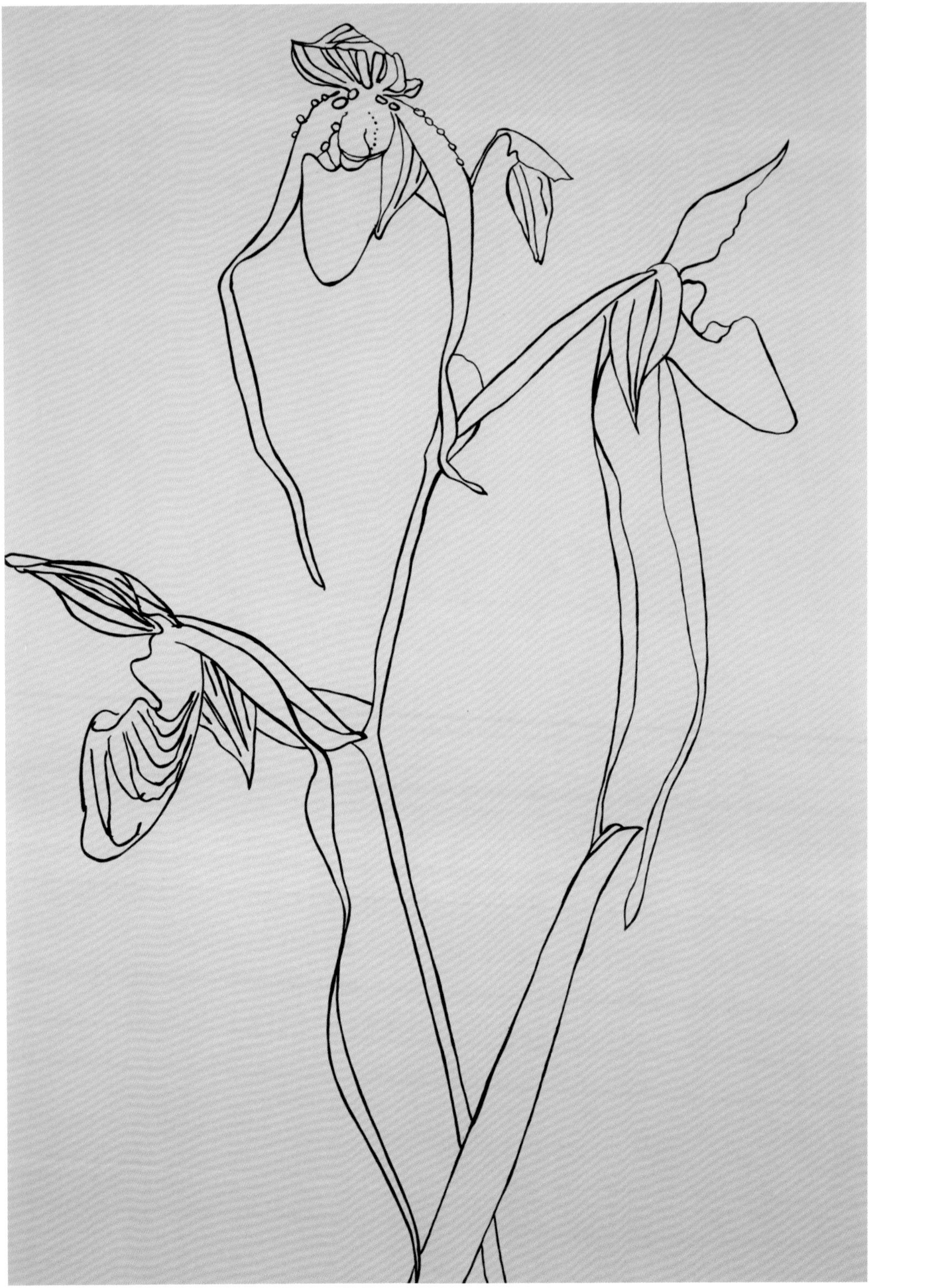

GARY HUME (born 1962)

Orchid

Gary Hume paints with high-gloss household paints on aluminium to achieve the smoothest, shiniest surface, where colour tones shift in different lights, and your reflection may be glimpsed, mirrored in a portrait or bewitched in pools of colour. Hume insists his work must be seen on the surface to retain its mystery: 'I don't want anyone going for a wander in the painting'. The slipper orchid, beautiful and menacing in its gleaming monotone and full of graceful movement, belongs with the *Water Series* of 1999, when Hume was the first YBA (Young British Artist) to represent Britain at the Venice Biennale. In these paintings, areas of shining reflective colour are covered in overlapping line drawings, mostly of female nudes. The circles of their breasts and nipples become repeat patterns of spirals (like pebbles thrown into water) and, where faces might be, their lips and eyes emerge among hanging lines of willow.

Hume graduated from Goldsmiths with the generation of Damien Hirst and took part in his challenging Freeze exhibition of 1988 in a redundant London warehouse. He achieved critical acclaim in the 1990s with his early paintings on aluminium known as *Hospital Doors*, several of which were bought by Charles Saatchi. Hume first reached the Royal Academy, where he is now a Fellow, as part of the legendary Sensation exhibition of 1997, which included a brilliant silhouette of cannabis leaves against a psychedelic background.

Hume's abstract blocks of shining colour are created and enlarged by a complicated process. First the outlines are traced onto acetate and projected onto a wall, rearranged, then transferred onto aluminium. Before the colours are brushed in, these outlines are built up with draught-excluder, which forms narrow dams between the different areas of paint. When the draught-excluder is later removed it leaves a clear metallic edge, like leading in stained glass. 'The edge', Hume says, 'is the only thing that matters' – and the lovely lines of the orchid, with its spots and stripes, echo this statement without explaining it.

Orchid (I) 1999
Gloss paint on aluminium panel,
96 x 66 cm
Collection of the artist

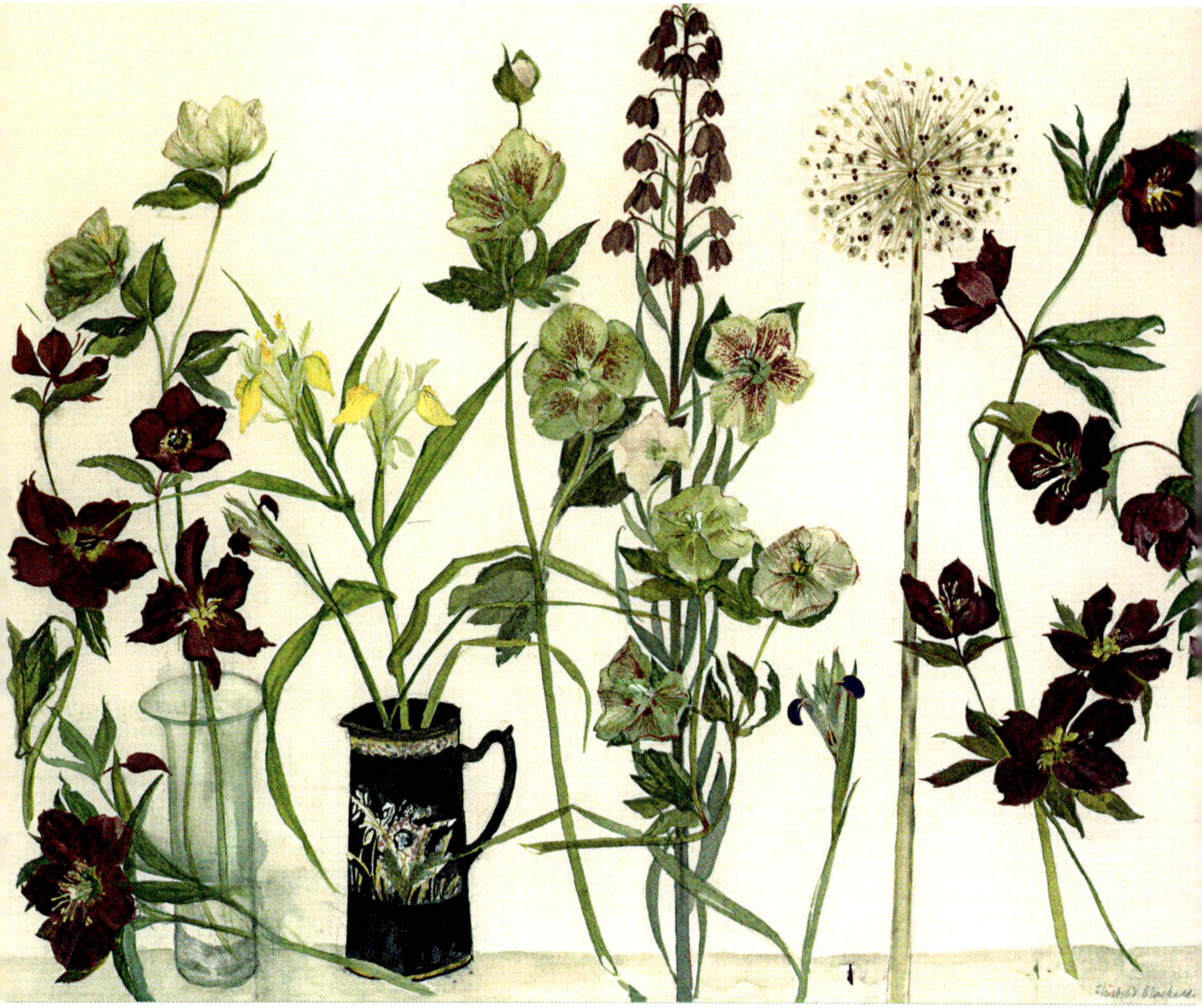

Hellebores and Other Flowers 2007
Watercolour on paper, 65 x 83 cm
Private collection

ELIZABETH BLACKADDER

(born 1931)

Hellebores and other flowers

Like many artists Elizabeth Blackadder would prefer to let her work speak for itself. The simple background facts consist of a lifetime spent in Edinburgh, teaching at the College of Art from 1962–86 and receiving increasing acclaim, especially for her flower paintings, on which her reputation has been mainly based since the 1960s. An early clue to the quality that makes these unique lies in her wartime childhood when she 'liked to press and draw flowers'. In many of her most exciting paintings the flowers are still lined up and arranged across the page as if they were pressed, but there is nothing flat or inanimate about them and their charm should not mask the mastery and refinement with which they are handled. Blackadder's visits to Japan during the 1980s provide another clue to the intriguing stylisation in her flower paintings, which are influenced by her admiration for Japanese taste, with its formality, delicacy and innate sense of pattern.

Sometimes Blackadder's paintings concentrate on one type of flower (favourites include irises, orchids and tulips), sometimes a whole range. The hellebores that dominate this painting are elegantly complemented by irises, a fritillary and an allium. The very pale greenish-pink hellebores come to life alongside the purple-black hellebores that frame them, and the flower-heads (that would all be inclined to hang downwards) are artfully tipped to show their lovely centres. Their greens and purples are repeated in two curious little snakeshead irises, known as *hermodactylus* (meaning the finger of Hermes, the Greek god who guided souls to the Underworld). A tall fritillary with flowers like a spire of purple bells is set almost like a signpost in the centre, alongside the round tracery of an allium seed head – and all these sombre colours are lightened by the bright yellow irises, glowing gently in their purple jug like candle flames. It is a masterpiece of design and harmony, its apparent simplicity is entirely deceptive and the flowers are larger than life in every sense.

INDEX

Artists whose flowers appear in the book are in *italic*

African sansevieria 65
African violet 12
allium 93
almond blossom 10
anemone 21, 29, 45, 61, 77
Arellano, Juan de 21
Art Nouveau 45, 63
artichoke 81
arum 7, 83

Bell, Vanessa 67, 81
bistort 25
Blackadder, Elizabeth 11, 93
blackthorn 63
blossom 10, 29, 35, 41, 45, 47, 63
Bosschaert, Ambrosius 12, 17
Botticelli, Sandro 7
bougainvillea 49
bramble 23
Brueghel, Jan 11, 19, 21, 23

Caillebotte, Gustave 10, 51
carnation 21, 23, 79
Cézanne, Paul 55, 67, 75, 77, 81
Chardin, Jean Baptiste Siméon 41
chestnut blossom 47
Christian symbolism (see also Vanitas) 7–8, 15, 23, 89
chrysanthemum 10, 45, 51, 55
columbine 15
cornflower 47
cowslip 15
Cubism 71, 75
cyclamen 11,12, 19

da Vinci, Leonardo 79
dahlia 10, 39, 53, 57
Dali, Salvador 8, 13, 89
de Heem, Jan Davidz. 23
de Zurbaran, Francisco 8
delphinium/ larkspur 10, 21, 39, 53, 57, 85
Dürer, Albrecht 15

Expressionists 73

Fantin-Latour, Henri 53
Fauves 65, 69, 77
fritillary/Crown imperial 17, 29, 93

Gauguin, Paul 11, 49, 67, 69, 77
geranium 25, 47, 61
gladiolus 53
Grant, Duncan 12, 67, 81
guelder rose 23, 25

Heade, Martin Johnson 7, 37
hellebore 93
Heron, Patrick 12
Hiroshige, Utagawa 10, 35
Hodgkin, Howard 13
Hokusai, Katsushika 33
hollyhock 25
honeysuckle 23, 29, 45
Hume, Gary 7, 91
hyacinth 19, 29

Impressionism 10, 39, 41, 47, 49, 51, 53, 55
iris 15, 19, 21, 25, 35, 83, 85, 93

Jack-in-the-pulpit 7, 83
Jiang Yu 31

Kandinsky, Wassily 12, 71
Klee, Paul 8, 71

lily 21, 27, 69, 83
lotus 13, 59, 65

Mackintosh, Charles Rennie 11, 63
Manet, Edouard 8, 39, 41, 53, 75
marigold 47, 53
Marvel of Peru 33
Matisse, Henri 11, 12, 57, 61, 65, 67, 69, 75, 77, 81
Merian, Maria Sybilla 27
Mignon, Abraham 8, 25
Millet, Jean-François 89
Monet, Claude 10-11, 39, 51, 59
morning glory 25, 27
Morris, Cedric 85
Morris, William 45

narcissus/daffodil 19, 29
Nicholson, Winifred 79
nigella 25
Nolde, Emil 73
North, Marianne 7, 43

O'Keeffe, Georgia 7, 83
orchid 7, 37, 43, 51, 91, 93

peony 15, 23, 27, 29, 31, 49
Peploe, Samuel 75
physalis 25
Picasso, Pablo 11, 57, 65, 67, 79, 81
pink 79
plum blossom 10
poppy 21, 23, 25, 29, 39, 47, 61, 73, 83, 85
primula/cowslip/auricula 15, 19, 29

quince 29
Quinn, Marc 8

red hot poker 81, 85
Redon, Odilon 61, 77
Renoir, Pierre-Auguste 10, 39, 51, 53
Rivera, Diego 7
rose 7–8, 13, 19, 21, 23, 25, 27, 29, 41, 45, 53, 63, 71, 75, 83, 89
Rousseau, Henri 65
Ruysch, Rachel 27

Schongauer, Martin 15
Scottish Colourists 75
Seghers, Daniel 21
Sisley, Alfred 39
Smith, Matthew 69
snapdragon 21
snowdrop 13, 19
Spencer, Stanley 13
sunflower 47, 87
Surrealists 61, 65, 69, 87, 89
Symbolists 49, 57, 61, 69

Tanning, Dorothea 13, 87
tulip 12, 17, 19, 21, 23, 25, 29, 45, 67, 93
Twombly, Cy 7

Van Gogh, Vincent 10, 47, 73, 77
van Huysum, Jan 8, 29
Vanitas symbols 17, 19, 25, 27
viola 19

wallflower 13
water lily 10-11, 59
wisteria 11
Wood, Christopher 79

yucca 65

ACKNOWLEDGEMENTS

The Publishers would like to thank those listed below for permission to reproduce the artworks illustrated in this book and for supplying photographs. Every care has been taken to trace copyright holders. Any copyright holders we have been unable to reach are invited to contact the publishers so that a full acknowledgment may be given in subsequent editions.

pages 2, 28 © Wallace Collection, London / Bridgeman Art Library page 6 © 2012 National Gallery of Art, Washington DC page 8 National Gallery, London / akg-images pages 9, 24 Fitzwilliam Museum, University of Cambridge / Bridgeman Art Library page 12 Peter Willi / © Succession H. Matisse / DACS 2012 / Bridgeman Art Library page 13 © The Estate of Stanley Spencer 2012, all rights reserved / DACS / Photo Agnew's, London / Bridgeman Art Library page 16 © John Mitchell Fine Paintings / Bridgeman Art Library page 18 Fitzwilliam Museum, University of Cambridge / Bridgeman Art Library page 20 Courtesy of Thomas Brod and Patrick Pilkington / Bridgeman Art Library page 22 Fitzwilliam Museum, University of Cambridge / Bridgeman Art Library page 26 © Museumslandschaft Hessen Kassel / Arno Hensmanns / Bridgeman Art Library page 30 School of Oriental and African Studies, University of London / Bridgeman Art Library page 32 Museum of Fine Art, Boston / William Sturgis Bigelow Collection / Bridgeman Art Library page 34 Fitzwilliam Museum, University of Cambridge / Bridgeman Art Library page 36 Photo Christie's Images / Bridgeman Art Library page 42 © RBGKew page 44 William Morris Gallery, London Borough of Waltham Forest page 52 Photo © Christie's Images / Bridgeman Art Library page 54 The Barnes Foundation, Philadelphia / Bridgeman Art Library pages 56, 57 © Succession Picasso / DACS 2012 page 60 Gemeentemuseum, The Hague / Bridgeman Art Library page 62 Photo © The Fine Art Society, London / Bridgeman Art Library page 64 Norton Simon Collection, Pasadena / Bridgeman Art Library page 66 © Estate of Duncan Grant, all rights reserved / DACS 2012 / Southampton City Art Gallery / Bridgeman Art Library page 68 Leeds Museums and Galleries / Bridgeman Art Library / Courtesy Alice Kadel page 72 © Nolde Stiftung Seebuell page 74 Photo © Christie's Images / Bridgeman Art Library page 76 Giraudon / © Succession H. Matisse / DACS 2012 / Bridgeman Art Library page 80 © Henrietta Garnett / Bridgeman Art Library page 81 © Tate, London 2012 page 82 © 2012 National Gallery of Art, Washington DC page 84 © Cedric Morris Estate / Tate, London 2012 page 86 © ADAGP, Paris and DACS, London 2012 / Tate, London 2012 page 88 © Salvador Dalí, Fundació Gala-Salvador Dalí / DACS 2012 page 90 © Gary Hume / Photo Stephen White / Courtesy White Cube page 92 © Elizabeth Blackadder

CELIA FISHER is an art historian and the author of *Flowers of the Renaissance* and a number of books on the flowers to be found in medieval illuminations. She is a passionate gardener with a painter's eye for shape and colour. Although she lectures widely on art, it is flower paintings and the artists who painted them that are her chief love. She lives just by Kew Gardens in London.